"This series is a tremendous resource for those wanting to study and teach the Bible with an understanding of how the gospel is woven throughout Scripture. Here are gospel-minded pastors and scholars doing gospel business from all the Scriptures. This is a biblical and theological feast preparing God's people to apply the entire Bible to all of life with heart and mind wholly committed to Christ's priorities."

BRYAN CHAPELL, President Emeritus, Covenant Theological Seminary

"Mark Twain may have smiled when he wrote to a friend, 'I didn't have time to write you a short letter, so I wrote you a long letter.' But the truth of Twain's remark remains serious and universal, because well-reasoned, compact writing requires extra time and extra hard work. And this is what we have in the Crossway Bible study series *Knowing the Bible*. The skilled authors and notable editors provide the contours of each book of the Bible as well as the grand theological themes that bind them together as one Book. Here, in a 12-week format, are carefully wrought studies that will ignite the mind and the heart."

R. KENT HUGHES, Senior Pastor Emeritus, College Church, Wheaton, Illinois

"*Knowing the Bible* brings together a gifted team of Bible teachers to produce a high-quality series of study guides. The coordinated focus of these materials is unique: biblical content, provocative questions, systematic theology, practical application, and the gospel story of God's grace presented all the way through Scripture."

PHILIP G. RYKEN, President, Wheaton College

"These *Knowing the Bible* volumes provide a significant and very welcome variation on the general run of inductive Bible studies. This series provides substantial instruction, as well as teaching through the very questions that are asked. *Knowing the Bible* then goes even further by showing how any given text links with the gospel, the whole Bible, and the formation of theology. I heartily endorse this orientation of individual books to the whole Bible and the gospel, and I applaud the demonstration that sound theology was not something invented later by Christians, but is right there in the pages of Scripture."

GRAEME L. GOLDSWORTHY, former lecturer, Moore Theological College; author, *According to Plan*, *Gospel and Kingdom*, *The Gospel in Revelation*, and *Gospel and Wisdom*

"What a gift to earnest, Bible-loving, Bible-searching believers! The organization and structure of the Bible study format presented through the *Knowing the Bible* series is so well conceived. Students of the Word are led to understand the content of passages through perceptive, guided questions, and they are given rich insights and application all along the way in the brief but illuminating sections that conclude each study. What potential growth in depth and breadth of understanding these studies offer! One can only pray that vast numbers of believers will discover more of God and the beauty of his Word through these rich studies."

BRUCE A. WARE, Professor of Christian Theology, The Southern Baptist Theological Seminary

KNOWING THE BIBLE

J. I. Packer, Theological Editor
Dane C. Ortlund, Series Editor
Lane T. Dennis, Executive Editor

• • • • • •

Genesis	Psalms	Jonah, Micah, and Nahum	Ephesians
Exodus	Proverbs		Philippians
Leviticus	Ecclesiastes	Haggai, Zechariah, and Malachi	Colossians and Philemon
Numbers	Song of Solomon		
Deuteronomy	Isaiah	Matthew	1–2 Thessalonians
Joshua	Jeremiah	Mark	1–2 Timothy and Titus
Judges	Lamentations, Habakkuk, and Zephaniah	Luke	
Ruth and Esther		John	Hebrews
1–2 Samuel		Acts	James
1–2 Kings	Ezekiel	Romans	1–2 Peter and Jude
1–2 Chronicles	Daniel	1 Corinthians	1–3 John
Ezra and Nehemiah	Hosea	2 Corinthians	Revelation
Job	Joel, Amos, and Obadiah	Galatians	

• • • • • •

J. I. PACKER is Board of Governors' Professor of Theology at Regent College (Vancouver, BC). Dr. Packer earned his DPhil at the University of Oxford. He is known and loved worldwide as the author of the best-selling book *Knowing God*, as well as many other titles on theology and the Christian life. He serves as the General Editor of the ESV Bible and as the Theological Editor for the *ESV Study Bible*.

LANE T. DENNIS is President of Crossway, a not-for-profit publishing ministry. Dr. Dennis earned his PhD from Northwestern University. He is Chair of the ESV Bible Translation Oversight Committee and Executive Editor of the *ESV Study Bible*.

DANE C. ORTLUND is Executive Vice President of Bible Publishing and Bible Publisher at Crossway. He is a graduate of Covenant Theological Seminary (MDiv, ThM) and Wheaton College (BA, PhD). Dr. Ortlund has authored several books and scholarly articles in the areas of Bible, theology, and Christian living.

MARK

A 12-WEEK STUDY

Dane C. Ortlund

:: CROSSWAY®

WHEATON, ILLINOIS

Trade paperback ISBN: 978-1-4335-3371-6
PDF ISBN: 978-1-4335-3438-6
MobiPocket ISBN: 978-1-4335-3439-3
EPub ISBN: 978-1-4335-3440-9

Crossway is a publishing ministry of Good News Publishers.

VP		28	27	26	25	24	23	22	21	20	19	18
17	16	15	14	13	12	11	10	9	8	7	6	5

TABLE OF CONTENTS

SERIES PREFACE

KNOWING THE BIBLE, as the series title indicates, was created to help readers know and understand the meaning, the message, and the God of the Bible. Each volume in the series consists of 12 units that progressively take the reader through a clear, concise study of that book of the Bible. In this way, any given volume can fruitfully be used in a 12-week format either in group study, such as in a church-based context, or in individual study. Of course, these 12 studies could be completed in fewer or more than 12 weeks, as convenient, depending on the context in which they are used.

Each study unit gives an overview of the text at hand before digging into it with a series of questions for reflection or discussion. The unit then concludes by highlighting the gospel of grace in each passage ("Gospel Glimpses"), identifying whole-Bible themes that occur in the passage ("Whole-Bible Connections"), and pinpointing Christian doctrines that are affirmed in the passage ("Theological Soundings").

The final component to each unit is a section for reflecting on personal and practical implications from the passage at hand. The layout provides space for recording responses to the questions proposed, and we think readers need to do this to get the full benefit of the exercise. The series also includes definitions of key words. These definitions are indicated by a note number in the text and are found at the end of each chapter.

Lastly, to help understand the Bible in this deeper way, we urge readers to use the ESV Bible and the *ESV Study Bible*, which are available in various print and digital formats, including online editions at www.esv.org. The *Knowing the Bible* series is also available online.

May the Lord greatly bless your study as you seek to know him through knowing his Word.

J. I. Packer
Lane T. Dennis

WEEK 1: OVERVIEW

▲

The Gospel of Mark plays a unique and strategic role in the Christian Bible. In this account of the life, death, and resurrection of Christ, we see him fulfilling in himself the Old Testament hopes for a coming king, the Messiah,[1] yet we also see the stark ways in which Jesus confounds public expectations of what this king will do: he will suffer. Mark's Gospel also gives us a vivid portrayal of what authentic discipleship[2] looks like for those who follow a rejected king.

Of the four Gospels, Mark was probably the first one written. It is the shortest and also the fastest-paced Gospel account. For example, Mark repeatedly transitions to a new section of his narrative with the word "immediately." While Matthew and Luke share quite a bit of material with Mark, Matthew and Luke contain large blocks of behavioral teaching by Jesus that Mark does not include. This absence gives Mark a feel of heightened intensity as events rapidly hurtle toward the final week of Jesus' earthly life.

Mark's Gospel is concerned with presenting Jesus as the Messiah, the king, the Son of David, who is rejected by the religious authorities and calls his followers to radical discipleship in the kingdom of God.[3] (For further background, see the *ESV Study Bible*, pages 1889–1892; also online at www.esv.org.)

▶ Placing It in the Larger Story

While Matthew focuses on Jesus as the Jewish Messiah, Luke describes Jesus as the one who welcomes the outsider, and John emphasizes Jesus as the eternal Son of God, Mark focuses on Jesus as the one who ushers in the kingdom of God. Through his life and teaching, but especially through his death and resurrection, Jesus fulfills all the Old Testament hopes and promises, bringing in the long expected new age.

▶ Key Verse

"Jesus came into Galilee, proclaiming the gospel of God, and saying, 'The time is fulfilled, and the kingdom of God is at hand; repent and believe in the gospel.'" (Mark 1:14–15)

▶ Date and Historical Background

Mark wrote his account of Jesus in perhaps the mid- to late-50s AD. He probably relied heavily on the eyewitness account of the apostle Peter. Though written in Rome, Mark's Gospel was aimed at the wider church, especially those who had not been raised as Jews, as is evident from the way Mark at times explains Jewish customs.

Mark wrote roughly 25 years after the death and resurrection of Jesus. At the time of writing, Nero was emperor in Rome, Paul was in the midst of his third missionary journey (Acts 18:23–21:16), and Jerusalem was about ten years away from being besieged by the Romans under the leadership of Vespasian and his son Titus (66–70 AD.).

▶ Outline

I. Introduction (1:1–15)

II. Demonstration of Jesus' Authority in Ministry (1:16–8:26)

    A. Jesus' early Galilean ministry (1:16–3:12)

    B. Jesus' later Galilean ministry (3:13–6:6)

        1. Calling of the Twelve (3:13–35)
        2. Parables (4:1–34)
        3. Nature miracle, exorcism, and healing (4:35–5:43)
        4. Rejection at Nazareth (6:1–6)

C. Work beyond Galilee (6:7–8:26)

    1. Sending of the Twelve (6:7–13)
    2. Death of John the Baptist (6:14–56)
    3. Teachings on moral defilement (7:1–23)
    4. Opening the door of grace to Gentiles (7:24–30)
    5. Additional miracles in Decapolis and Bethsaida (7:31–8:26)

III. Demonstration of Jesus' Authority in Suffering (8:27–16:8)

A. Journey to Jerusalem (8:27–10:52)

    1. Peter's confession (8:27–33)
    2. Call to discipleship (8:34–9:1)
    3. Transfiguration and healing (9:2–29)
    4. Instruction on discipleship: putting others first (9:30–50)
    5. Instruction on discipleship: divorce, wealth, humility (10:1–52)

B. Entering and judging Jerusalem (11:1–13:37)

    1. Triumphal entry into Jerusalem (11:1–11)
    2. Jesus' judgment on religious leaders (11:12–12:44)
    3. Jesus and the coming universal judgment (13:1–37)

C. Death and resurrection in Jerusalem (14:1–16:8)

    1. Betrayal (14:1–52)
    2. Trial (14:53–15:20)
    3. Crucifixion and resurrection (15:21–16:8)
    4. ["Longer ending of Mark" (16:9–20; see note)]

▶ As You Get Started . . .

What is your general understanding of the role of Mark's Gospel related to the other three Gospels? Do you have any sense of what Mark uniquely contributes?

How do you understand Mark's contribution to Christian theology? From your current knowledge of Mark, what does this account of the life of Jesus teach us about God, humanity, sin, redemption, and other doctrines?

What has perplexed you about Mark's Gospel? Are there any confusing parts to this Gospel that you hope to resolve as you begin this study of Mark?

As You Finish This Unit . . .

Take a moment now to ask for the Lord's blessing and help as you engage in this study of Mark. And take a moment also to look back through this unit of study, to reflect on a few key things that the Lord may be teaching you—and perhaps to highlight or underline these to review again in the future.

Definitions

[1] **Messiah** – Transliteration of a Hebrew word meaning "anointed one," the equivalent of the Greek word *Christ*. "Anointed one" signified kingship. The Messiah therefore came to mean the anticipated coming king who would liberate Israel once and for all and bring in the kingdom of God. Jesus affirmed that he was the Messiah sent from God (Matt. 16:16–17).

[2] **Discipleship** – Submitting to the teachings of another and following that person's way of life. In the NT, disciples were those who submitted themselves to the teaching of Jesus, especially the twelve men who traveled and lived with Jesus during his earthly ministry.

[3] **Kingdom of God** – The rule of God manifested in the long-awaited restoration of his people and indeed the whole world, in which God would reign under the glad submission of all people. When Jesus came two thousand years ago, he announced that the kingdom of God had arrived (Mark 1:15; Luke 17:20–21). Yet because of ongoing rebellion and rejection of Jesus and his rule, the kingdom still awaits its final consummation and fulfillment in Jesus' second coming (Mark 14:25). For this reason we pray for the kingdom to come (Matt. 6:10).

Week 2: Introduction

Mark 1:1–20

The Place of the Passage

This opening passage of Mark sets the stage for the rest of the Gospel. Mark starts with the words, "The beginning of the gospel of Jesus Christ" (1:1). Mark is writing, above all else, about the gospel, as the first words out of Jesus' mouth reiterate: "The time is fulfilled, and the kingdom of God is at hand; repent and believe in the gospel" (1:15). What is the gospel? Mark explains that it is the good news of the fulfillment of God's promises, and the rest of Mark will show how Jesus fulfills yet transforms Old Testament hopes, especially the hope for a coming king.

The Big Picture

Mark 1:1–20 shows us the good news that Jesus came as the fulfillment of all the promises of the Old Testament.

Reflection and Discussion

Read through the complete passage for this study, Mark 1:1–20. Then review the shorter passages below and write your own notes on the following questions—first with regard to John the Baptist (vv. 1–9) and then with regard to Jesus (vv. 9–20). (For further background, see the *ESV Study Bible*, pages 1893–1894; also available online at www.esv.org.)

1. The Ministry of John the Baptist (1:1–9)

In the first verse of his Gospel Mark indicates what is driving him to write, and then immediately quotes the Old Testament as he begins writing. What do these opening few verses teach us about why Mark is writing and the roles both John the Baptist and Jesus play in this?

Many scholars believe Mark introduces Jesus as bringing about a new "exodus"[1] for the people of God, similar to the liberation from Egypt in the book of Exodus. This is because Mark frequently seems to allude to passages in Isaiah in which God promises a new "exodus" to his people (e.g., Isa. 11:11–16; 40:3–11; 42:16; 43:2, 5–7, 16–19; 48:20–49:11; 51:10). What in Mark 1:1–13 might lead to this conclusion?

There are several similarities between Isaiah 40:1–3 and the way Mark presents John the Baptist. What are some of them?

Untying the straps of sandals can be the responsibility of a low servant, but it was something that a Jewish person was not supposed to do. What does this tell us about John's statement in Mark 1:7?

John says that the one coming after him "will baptize you with the Holy Spirit"[2] (1:8). We know from Mark 1:2–3 that Mark sees his Gospel account as building on the Old Testament, so what might Mark have in mind in verse 8? For clarification read Isaiah 32:15, 44:3, Ezekiel 11:18–19, and Joel 2:28. Note also what happens with the Spirit in Mark 1:10.

2. The Ministry of Jesus (1:9–20)

Jesus comes to the Jordan River and is baptized[3] by John. John himself has already made it clear that Jesus is greater than he is, so this cannot be an act of submission to John. Instead Jesus is likely identifying with the people. How might later statements by Jesus, such as Mark 10:45, further fill out the significance of Jesus' baptism?

With the descent of the Spirit, Jesus is commissioned for unique service (note Isa. 11:2; 42:1; 61:1). In light of the way Mark views Jesus as the fulfillment of the Old Testament, what is the significance of this? Others had been commissioned for unique service to God in the past—Adam, for instance, or Israel. How is Jesus both similar to and different from these other servants? How does the temptation of Jesus in the wilderness by Satan[4] reinforce the connection between Jesus and other Old Testament servants of God? Where else in Scripture do we see a servant of God being tempted by Satan while "with the wild animals" (Mark 1:13)?

Mark 1:14–15 is a sort of summary statement of Mark's whole Gospel. Here we see that "the kingdom of God is at hand." God has done this by bringing history to a climax ("the time is fulfilled"), yet at the same time people are called to respond in a certain way ("repent and believe"). What do we learn of the nature of the kingdom of God here? How does this differ from popular expectations of the Jews at this time regarding what the coming of God's kingdom would look like, as they visualized the kingdom in terms of political liberation from Roman rule?

In 1:16–20 Jesus calls the first four disciples. Read Jeremiah 16:15–17 and consider what it meant for Jesus to call these four men to be "fishers of men" (Mark 1:17).

What do we learn from verses 18 and 20 about the nature of Christian discipleship?

Read through the following three sections on *Gospel Glimpses*, *Whole-Bible Connections*, and *Theological Soundings*. Then take time to reflect on the *Personal Implications* these sections may have for your walk with the Lord.

▶ Gospel Glimpses

GOOD NEWS AT ITS CORE. While the Bible is filled with commands, and these commands must unquestionably be heeded by believers, the overarching story line of the Bible is one of rescue and deliverance—of gospel. The message of the Bible, at its core, is what has been done by God in Christ for sinners, as the first verse of Mark underscores: "The beginning of the gospel of Jesus Christ, the Son of God." Mark wrote to recount good news. His Gospel relates what God has done for us in Jesus.

THE PROMISE-KEEPING GOD. In Mark's focus on Jesus as the fulfillment of Old Testament expectations, we see the grace[5] of God in his commitment to keep his promises to his people, despite their waywardness. "I will be your God, and you shall be my people" was a constant refrain throughout the Old Testament (e.g., Ex. 6:7; Lev. 26:12; Jer. 7:23). Yet God's people were consistently faithless. God sent his own Son, however, to do what his people had always failed to do. Although Adam and Israel were both God's "son," to neither of them could God finally say, "with you I am well pleased" (Mark 1:11). Those who are in Christ, however, can be fully assured that God is "well pleased" with them, because they have been covered by Christ's righteousness and adopted into God's family as his very children. God keeps his promises.

CALLING THE ORDINARY. We also see the grace of God in the calling of the first four disciples. Peter, Andrew, James, and John did nothing to seek out Jesus. Jesus sought *them* out. Indeed, not only is the initiative totally on the side of Jesus, but Jesus goes to blue-collar, untrained fishermen to begin to build his church. Here, as throughout the Bible, God in his grace chooses the weak things of the world to shame the strong (1 Cor. 1:27).

Whole-Bible Connections

SON OF GOD. In Mark 1:1 Jesus is called "the Son of God." One layer of meaning here may highlight the deity of Christ: Jesus is God's Son in that he is himself God. Another layer of meaning, however, connects the title "Son of God" in Mark 1:1 with a whole-Bible trajectory. Adam was "the son of God" (Luke 3:38). Adam failed, however, to walk in obedience to God. God later called Israel to be his "son," and the Bible even describes God as calling Israel his "firstborn" (Ex. 4:22–23). Yet Israel, too, failed. Jesus, however, was the final Son of God, the true Firstborn, the Son who succeeded where all others had failed (Mark 1:11). Because of his obedient sonship, God is pleased to adopt into his own family those who are united to the Son by faith (Rom. 8:14–17; Heb. 2:10). Mark 1 taps into this whole-Bible theme.

WILDERNESS TESTING. Immediately after his baptism, Jesus is driven by the Spirit into the wilderness, where he is tested for 40 days. This picks up a theme that travels through the Old Testament: Moses spent 40 days on barren Mount Sinai (Ex. 34:28); Israel was tested for 40 years in the desert (Deut. 8:2); and Elijah spent 40 days in the desert, too (1 Kings 19:8). In each case the "wilderness" experience was a testing ground of sorts.

KINGDOM OF GOD. Jesus' first words in Mark are, "The time is fulfilled, and the kingdom of God is at hand; repent and believe in the gospel" (1:15). The coming of the kingdom of God means that God's rule over people's hearts and lives is being established in and through Jesus. The kingdom is a whole-Bible theme in that Eden was set up as a little "kingdom" of God with Adam, the first king, commissioned to rule over the earth (Gen. 1:28). The king theme is heightened with the setting up of the kingship in Israel, and especially with David, to whom God promises a lasting dynasty (2 Sam. 7:8–16). With Jesus this kingdom dawns decisively, and he will one day bring this kingdom to completion, sitting on his throne for all the world to see (Rev. 4:1–11).

Theological Soundings

DEITY OF CHRIST. Jesus is "the Son of God" (Mark 1:1), not only in that he is the one called by God to rule the earth as God's representative, but also in that he *is* God. This is reinforced in Mark 1:3, where "prepare the way of the Lord" (Isa. 40:3) originally referred to Yahweh but is applied by Mark to Jesus. The New Testament teaches that Jesus is included in the divine identity (1 Cor. 8:6; Rom. 9:5; Col. 1:15–20; Heb. 1:3). While there are distinctions of persons within the one Godhead, Jesus Christ is as much God as God the Father and God the Holy Spirit.

TRINITY. In Mark 1:9–11, Jesus is baptized. We are told that the Spirit descended on him like a dove, and a voice from heaven affirmed Jesus' sonship. We see here all three persons of the Trinity—Father, Son, and Spirit. Broadly speaking, Christian theology teaches that the Father orchestrates salvation, the Son accomplishes salvation, and the Spirit applies salvation.

SALVATION. "Repent and believe in the gospel" (Mark 1:15). Repentance and faith (*faith* is the noun form of the Greek word translated *believe*) are the two basic motions on the part of the believer in receiving Christian salvation. Throughout the New Testament these two are linked (e.g., Acts 20:21; Heb. 6:1). We might say faith and repentance are two sides of the single coin of salvation. In repentance we turn from sin; in faith we turn to God.

> ## Personal Implications

Take time to reflect on the implications of Mark 1 for your own life today. Make notes below on the personal implications for your walk with the Lord of (1) the *Gospel Glimpses*, (2) the *Whole-Bible Connections*, (3) the *Theological Soundings*, and (4) this passage as a whole.

1. Gospel Glimpses

2. Whole-Bible Connections

3. Theological Soundings

----

4. Mark 1:1–20

> ## As You Finish This Unit . . .

Take a moment now to ask for the Lord's blessing and help as you continue in this study of Mark. And take a moment also to look back through this unit of study, to reflect on a few key things that the Lord may be teaching you—and perhaps to highlight or underline these to review again in the future.

Definitions

[1] **The exodus** – The departure of the people of Israel from Egypt and their journey to Mount Sinai under Moses' leadership (Exodus 1–19; Numbers 33). The exodus demonstrated God's power and providence for his people, who had been enslaved by the Egyptians. The annual festival of Passover commemorates God's final plague upon the Egyptians, resulting in Israel's release from Egypt.

[2] **Holy Spirit** – One of the persons of the Trinity, and thus fully God. The Bible mentions several roles of the Holy Spirit, including convicting people of sin, bringing them to conversion, indwelling them and empowering them to live in Christlike righteousness and service, supporting them in times of trial, and enabling them to understand the Scriptures. The Holy Spirit was poured out at Pentecost in Acts 2 in fulfillment of Old Testament prophecy (e.g., Ezek. 36:26–27). The Spirit was vitally active in Jesus' life and ministry on earth (e.g., Luke 3:22).

[3] **Baptize** – Literally "to immerse" or "to wash." Refers to the Christian practice of immersing a new believer in water as an outward sign of the inward reality of regeneration. This regeneration is the work of the Holy Spirit (see John 3:5, 8; Titus 3:5). Considerable disagreement exists as to the method of baptism (i.e., sprinkling vs. immersion) and who may be baptized (i.e., believers only vs. believers and their infant children).

[4] **Satan** – A spiritual being whose name means "accuser." As the leader of all the demonic forces, he opposes God's rule and seeks to harm God's people and accuse them of wrongdoing. His power, however, is confined to the bounds that God has set for him, and one day he will be destroyed along with all his demons (Matt. 25:41; Rev. 20:10).

[5] **Grace** – Unmerited favor, especially the free gift of salvation that God gives to believers through faith in Jesus Christ.

Week 3: Jesus' Early Galilean Ministry

Mark 1:21–3:12

▲

The Place of the Passage

Having called the first four disciples, Jesus begins his ministry. In these opening chapters his ministry is one of both word and deed. Mark recounts how Jesus preaches and teaches, and also how Jesus has authority over demons and sickness. These first three chapters contribute to the broader theme of the first half of Mark (1:1–8:26), which is the kingly authority of Jesus, the widespread amazement, and positive reception Jesus receives.

The Big Picture

Mark 1:21–3:12 shows us that Jesus possesses unrivalled authority in both his teaching and his deeds.

> ### Reflection and Discussion

This section of Mark contains a number of fast-moving accounts of various events in the early ministry of Jesus. In Mark 2 we see Jesus begin to receive opposition from the religious leaders. We will therefore organize this section under the two headings "Jesus' Authority Revered" and "Jesus' Authority Challenged." Read Mark 1:21–3:12 and consider the following questions. (For further background, see the *ESV Study Bible*, pages 1895–1898; also available online at www.esv.org.)

1. Jesus' Authority Revered (1:21–45)

The very first thing Jesus does in his earthly ministry is enter the synagogue[1] and teach. What does this tell us about Jesus' goals in his earthly ministry?

Read Mark 1:22 and 1:27. What is Mark showing us about Jesus in this opening event of Jesus' ministry?

Jesus' healing ministry in Mark 1:29–34 shows us his great compassion. These healings also tell us something about who Jesus is and why he came. In light of Jesus' earlier statement in Mark 1:15 that "the kingdom of God is at hand," how do we see this kingdom advancing in verses 29–34? How might we relate this healing ministry to the events of Genesis 1–3? Consider Mark 1:34 in light of Adam and his failure to exorcise Satan from the Garden of Eden.

Mark 1:35 uses four verbs in describing Jesus' actions one day—rising, departed, went, prayed. What does this tell us about Jesus' priorities in his ministry? What can we learn from this for our own walk with God?

In first-century Palestine, a leper[2] was someone who was not only physically unclean but also ceremonially unclean. To touch such uncleanness would make oneself unclean. In Mark 1:40–45 Jesus heals a leper not simply by speaking to him but by touching him (v. 41). Doing so did not make Jesus unclean; it made the leper clean. What does this teach us about who Jesus is and what he came to do?

2. Jesus' Authority Challenged (2:1–3:12)

The first thing Jesus says to the paralytic who is brought to him has nothing to do with the paralysis: "Son, your sins are forgiven" (Mark 2:5). What does this tell us about the deepest problem—the deepest "paralysis"—needing healing, not only in the paralytic but in all of us?

In Mark 2:9, in response to the scribes' protests at Jesus' claim to forgive sins, Jesus asks which is easier—to tell the paralytic that his sins are forgiven, or to tell him to rise and walk? This is somewhat perplexing. Which *is* easier? How would you answer that? The point here is evidently that it is easier to *say*, "Your sins are forgiven," because it cannot be disproven. On a deeper level, however, it is in fact harder to proclaim forgiveness of sins, because only God can do that—as the scribes rightly understand. The logic here, then, is that since Jesus can do the visible miracle (heal the paralytic), this is evidence that he also has the power to do the invisible miracle (forgive sins).

Jewish tax collectors in New Testament times collaborated financially with Rome against their fellow Jews. What is the significance of Jesus calling Levi (Matthew) in Mark 2:13–14?

A further challenge to Jesus' authority comes in Mark 2:18–22, as the people ask why Jesus and his disciples do not fast. What is Jesus' answer? How do Old Testament passages such as Isaiah 62:5 and Hosea 2:19–20 clarify Jesus' answer?

In Mark 2:23–28 and 3:1–6 Jesus offends the Jewish religious leaders by doing on the Sabbath[3] what they considered unlawful. How does each of these events contribute to the portrait of Jesus that Mark is drawing? How does each demonstrate Jesus' unparalleled authority? In what way does Mark 3:7–12 then draw to a close this section of Mark describing Jesus' early Galilean ministry?

Read through the following three sections on *Gospel Glimpses, Whole-Bible Connections,* and *Theological Soundings*. Then take time to reflect on the *Personal Implications* these sections may have for your walk with the Lord.

Gospel Glimpses

CONTAGIOUS HOLINESS. In the Old Testament law, the uncleanness of leprosy was contagious. To touch such uncleanness was defiling. Unclean plus clean equaled unclean. In the Gospel of Mark, with the coming of the kingdom (Mark 1:15), this is turned inside out. Unclean plus clean equals clean. Defilement used to be contagious; with Jesus, holiness is contagious. This is meant to instruct not only lepers but all of us, for we are all, in the only sense that matters, unclean. Defiled *morally.* Unholy. Jesus brought with him a whole new way of thinking, a new mental universe in which we see ourselves not as basically clean but in danger of defilement, but as basically defiled and in need of cleansing. In Jesus that cleansing is available.

HOPE FOR SINNERS, NOT THE RIGHTEOUS. "Those who are well have no need of a physician, but those who are sick. I came not to call the righteous, but sinners" (Mark 2:17). Jesus did not come for the religious elite, the socially privileged. He came for the "tax collectors and sinners," with whom he ate (Mark 2:15). How could this be? The answer ultimately provided by Mark's Gospel is: Jesus, the one righteous person, allowed himself on the cross to be treated as a sinner, so that sinners could be treated as righteous as they place their faith in him. Martin Luther called this "the great exchange." To put it in terms of the healing of the leper: The only truly "clean" man who ever lived became unclean on the cross so that you and I, unclean, can be freely cleansed by simply asking for it. Or, as Paul would put it, God "made him to be sin who knew no sin, so that in him we might become the righteousness of God" (2 Cor. 5:21).

23

Whole-Bible Connections

SABBATH. Several of the events of Mark 1–3 take place on the Sabbath, climaxing in Jesus' declaration that he is "lord even of the Sabbath" (Mark 2:28). This statement reaches all the way back to creation, when God created the world in six days and rested on the seventh. His people were then instructed likewise to rest on the seventh day. This "rest" came to be identified with life in the Promised Land in the historical books of the Old Testament (Joshua—2 Chronicles). To enter the land was to enter rest. Yet even once they are in the land, true Sabbath rest remains elusive to God's people, as indicated by later texts such as Psalm 95. Only in Jesus is real Sabbath rest found (note Matt. 11:28–30), as the letter to the Hebrews draws out (Heb. 3:7–4:13). Jesus is indeed "lord even of the Sabbath."

SICKNESS AND HEALTH. With the fall in Eden, sickness, disease, and death entered the world. And when God gave his people the law, the curses resulting from disobedience included horrific sickness and disease (Deut. 28:22, 27, 35). Amid Israel's ongoing moral failure, the prophets longed for the day when true health would be restored in a renewed Eden (Isa. 35:5–6; Jer. 33:6; Ezek. 34:4, 16). In Jesus this day has dawned, and one day, at his second coming, Jesus will finish what he started in his earthly ministry, eradicating all sickness once and for all (Rev. 22:1–3).

BRIDEGROOM AND BRIDE. Jesus says in Mark 2:19 that his disciples do not fast because "the bridegroom is with them." Referring to himself in this way, Jesus links up with a whole-Bible theme in which God's relationship with his people is likened to a husband's relationship to his wife (e.g., Isa. 54:5; Jer. 2:1–2; 3:20; Hos. 2:16). Jesus is the ultimate bridegroom, loving his wife (the church) despite her faithlessness, to the point of dying for her (Eph. 5:25–32).

Theological Soundings

DEITY OF CHRIST. Christ's deity is underscored both explicitly and implicitly in this section of Mark. Explicitly, the demons fall down before Jesus and proclaim, "You are the Son of God." (Mark 3:11). Jesus does not deflect this but receives it and orders the demons not to make him known (3:12). Implicitly, the scribes who see Jesus pronounce forgiveness on the paralytic consider this blasphemy, reasoning, "Who can forgive sins but God alone?" (2:7). Jesus then goes on to heal the man, confirming by the healing that he is able to do what he says, not only in healing but also in forgiving.

SIN. Jesus scandalized the religious leaders of his day by eating with "many tax collectors and sinners" (Mark 2:15). Responding to the scribes' questioning of this practice, Jesus told them, "Those who are well have no need of a physician, but those who are sick. I came not to call the righteous, but sinners" (2:17). Jesus says this tongue in cheek—he came not to call those who *presumed* themselves righteous and who therefore felt no need for a Savior. In truth none are righteous (Rom. 3:9–18). All are in need of saving. What we learn of sin here is that sin manifests itself in two ways: sinful real unrighteousness (the tax collectors and sinners) and sinful bogus righteousness (the scribes and Pharisees).

Personal Implications

Take time to reflect on the implications of Mark 1:21–3:12 for your own life today. Make notes below on the personal implications for your walk with the Lord of (1) the *Gospel Glimpses*, (2) the *Whole-Bible Connections*, (3) the *Theological Soundings*, and (4) this passage as a whole.

1. Gospel Glimpses

2. Whole-Bible Connections

3. Theological Soundings

4. Mark 1:21–3:12

As You Finish This Unit . . .

Take a moment now to ask for the Lord's blessing and help as you continue in this study of Mark. And take a moment also to look back through this unit of study, to reflect on a few key things that the Lord may be teaching you—and perhaps to highlight or underline these to review again in the future.

Definitions

[1] **Synagogue** – In Jerusalem, worship took place at the temple. In cities other than Jerusalem, however, which had no temple, the synagogue (meaning "assembly") was the center of Jewish worship. Synagogues were located in most of the leading towns of Israel.

[2] **Leper** – A leper was someone suffering from leprosy, which was a term for a variety of related skin diseases, many of which were highly contagious. See Leviticus 13.

[3] **Sabbath** – For Jews the Sabbath is Saturday, the seventh day of the week, a day of worship and rest (Gen. 2:2–3; Ex. 31:13–17). Christians meet for worship on Sunday, the day of Christ's resurrection (Acts 20:7), and regard Sunday, rather than Saturday, as their weekly day of rest. Believers also look forward to an eternal Sabbath rest, won for them by Jesus (Heb. 4:1–16). See also "Sabbath" under the *Whole-Bible Connections* on page 24.

WEEK 4: JESUS' LATER GALILEAN MINISTRY

Mark 3:13–6:6

▲

In this section of Mark, Jesus' ministry and authority accelerate in new ways. After calling the twelve apostles (3:13–19), yet before sending them out (6:7–13), Jesus continues his teaching and healing ministry in ways that create heightened amazement at him—though also heightened opposition. The main effect of these chapters is to continue to develop the positive reception Jesus receives from the masses, which will come to a crashing halt halfway through Mark's Gospel.

The Big Picture

In Mark 3:13–6:6 Jesus demonstrates before the twelve disciples his unparalleled authority through teaching and healing.

Reflection and Discussion

Read through the complete passage for this study, Mark 3:13–6:6. Then review the two passages listed below and write your notes on the following questions concerning various events in the early ministry of Jesus, first by word (3:13–4:34) and then by deed (4:35–6:6). (For further background, see the *ESV Study Bible*, pages 1898–1904; also available online at www.esv.org.)

1. Jesus' Ministry by Word (3:13–4:34)

In Mark 3:13–18 Jesus calls the twelve disciples. Knowing that Mark views Jesus' coming as the fulfillment of Old Testament expectations, what might be the significance of Jesus choosing twelve men? Note Revelation 21:12–14.

"Whoever blasphemes[1] against the Holy Spirit never has forgiveness, but is guilty of an eternal sin" (Mark 3:29). Some have interpreted this to mean that there is a secret unpardonable sin which well-meaning followers of Christ might unwittingly fall into. In the context of Mark 3:22–29, however, it is clear that Jesus is not denying forgiveness to those who in contrition ask for it (note Mark 10:45). Rather, forgiveness is withheld from those who consistently attribute to Satan what is accomplished by the power of God—that is, if one makes a flagrant, willful judgment that the Spirit's testimony about Jesus is satanic.

How might we see such blasphemy against the Spirit today?

In what way does Jesus reconstitute or transform the community of faith in Mark 3:31–35?

The parables[2] in Mark's Gospel are concentrated in chapter 4. Here Jesus uses parables to explain what the kingdom of God is like. These parables prove to be not only instruction for those "inside" but also judgment for those "outside."

What is common to each of the first three seeds of the sower parable (4:15–19)? What is the central point of the parable (4:1–20)?

What is the main point of each of the next three parables—a lamp under a basket (4:21–25), a growing seed (4:26–29), and the mustard seed (4:30–34)? How do they contribute to Jesus' portrayal of what the kingdom of God is like?

---

2. Jesus' Ministry by Deed (4:35–6:6)

In Mark 4:35–41 we read a historical account of a boat that is caught up in a furious storm, resulting in great fear among those on board, only to be saved at the last moment by waking a man asleep within the boat. Where else have we heard such an account? For a hint see Matthew 12:38–42. In light of Job 12:15, 28:25, Psalm 33:7, and Psalm 107:25–30, what is the implication of Mark 4:39, and how might this explain the disciples' terror in verse 41?

The account that opens Mark 5 is striking, and not a typical instance of demon[3] possession. When asked his name by Jesus, the demon answers, "Legion, for we are many" (5:9). A legion was the largest unit of the Roman army, numbering up to six thousand soldiers. Evidently this is an unusually strong demon (or group of demons) that has taken hold of this man. What is Mark communicating to us about the mission and authority of Jesus through this account?

On his way to respond to the plea of Jairus, whose daughter is on the verge of death, Jesus is touched by a woman whose illness had rendered her ceremonially unclean. She would not have been able to worship at the temple in the section reserved for women, and would even have had to announce her uncleanness when in public. What does Jesus' attentive care for this woman reveal about who he is? How do we understand Jesus' agenda in light of the fact that healing this woman delays his visit to a young girl on death's doorstep? In 5:33 we learn of the fear this woman felt—where else in Mark have we heard of fear, and what is the relation of fear to faith in Mark 5:33–34?

What does the account of Jesus' rejection in his hometown in Mark 6:1–6 tell us about the relationship between his performance of miracles and the faith of the people?

_____

_____

_____

_____

_____

_____

_____

_____

_____

_____

Read through the following three sections on *Gospel Glimpses, Whole-Bible Connections,* and *Theological Soundings*. Then take time to reflect on the *Personal Implications* these sections may have for your walk with the Lord.

Gospel Glimpses

SUMMONED BY GRACE. "And he went up on the mountain and called to him those whom he desired" (Mark 3:13). Jesus' calling of his disciples is not related to any prior commitment or qualification on their part. It is solely at his invitation that they are summoned. The same holds true when God calls men and women to be his disciples today (see 1 Cor. 1:26–29).

THE SOURCE OF TRUE CLEANSING. As with the case of the leper in Mark 1:40–45, Jesus once more comes into physical contact with a ceremonially unclean person and instead of Jesus becoming unclean, the unclean person becomes clean (Mark 5:25–34). With Jesus, cleanliness, we might say, is contagious. Today, too, fellowship with him, communing with him, learning of him through the Word—all this does not make Jesus *less* holy but makes us, despite our sinfulness, *more* holy.

MORE THAN WE EVER ASKED. In Mark 5 Jairus asked Jesus to heal his daughter from a sickness. When Jesus showed up, however, she had already died, and Jesus did far more than Jairus ever asked. Jesus raised her from the dead. Jairus asked for a healing from sickness to health. Jesus provided a resurrection from death to life. Such is the heart of the Lord: he gives "far more abundantly than all that we ask or think" (Eph. 3:20).

Whole-Bible Connections

THE CALLING OF THE TWELVE. In the Old Testament, God called the line of Abraham, Isaac, and Jacob to be the family through whom he would work to restore the world. Jacob had twelve sons, each of whom became the head of one of what would eventually be the twelve tribes of Israel. In the New Testament, Jesus, God incarnate, also calls out twelve men to be his chosen ones through whom he would work to restore the world (Mark 3:13–19). We see here the unity of the Bible as Jesus carries on the work of God's people, begun in the Old Testament. Note also Revelation 21:9–17.

THE COSMIC TREE. In Mark 4:30–32 Jesus compares the kingdom of God to a tiny mustard seed which, when full grown, becomes the largest plant in the garden, in which the birds find rest and shade. This parable picks up an image carried through the Old Testament of a huge tree in whose branches the birds of the air nest and find shade (Ezek. 17:22–24; Dan. 4:10–23). Such a tree was proverbial in ancient literature, referring to the national superpower of the day, in whose shade the nations ("birds") nested. The embracing of the nations in the kingdom of God is therefore probably part of the significance of Jesus' parable in Mark 4. Also striking is the reversal that takes place, as the smallest seed provides a tree with the greatest branches (note also Ezek. 17:24). While the kingdom of God is outwardly unimpressive, the nations are gradually being gathered into it, and one day this kingdom will be unmistakably triumphant.

Theological Soundings

FORGIVENESS. "All sins will be forgiven the children of man, and whatever blasphemies they utter, but whoever blasphemes against the Holy Spirit never has forgiveness, but is guilty of an eternal sin" (Mark 3:28–29). If a person consistently attributes to Satan what is accomplished by God's power, such a person does not know God and will not receive forgiveness. For the people of God, however, Jesus' statement that "all sins will be forgiven the children of man" anticipates the eternally valid substitutionary atonement Jesus will be seen to provide in the final chapters of Mark's Gospel (note also 10:45).

THE WORD OF GOD. Jesus' parable of the sower in Mark 4:1–9, with his explanation of it in 4:13–20, centers on "the word"—in Mark, the message of the gospel (note 1:1, 14–15). The saving news of what God is doing in Jesus to restore the world impacts human hearts with very different results. Where the heart is receptive and welcoming to this message in a persevering way, this word bears fruit all out of proportion to what might be expected. The word of God, we learn in Mark 4, is powerful and fruitful, yet also dividing and alienating.

DEITY OF CHRIST. In Mark 4:35–41 Jesus calms a storm. Rather than being relieved, however, the disciples seem to be even more afraid of Jesus after the storm than they were of the storm itself! Why? In the Old Testament, it is God who calms the waves (Job 12:15; Ps. 33:7) and the storm (Job 28:25; Ps. 107:25–30; Amos 4:13). The disciples were coming to realize that their teacher was God himself in the flesh.

Personal Implications

Take time to reflect on the implications of Mark 3:13–6:6 for your own life today. Make notes below on the personal implications for your walk with the Lord of (1) the *Gospel Glimpses*, (2) the *Whole-Bible Connections*, (3) the *Theological Soundings*, and (4) this passage as a whole.

1. Gospel Glimpses

2. Whole-Bible Connections

3. Theological Soundings

4. Mark 3:13–6:6

As You Finish This Unit . . .

Take a moment now to ask for the Lord's blessing and help as you continue in this study of Mark. And take a moment also to look back through this unit of study, to reflect on a few key things that the Lord may be teaching you—and perhaps to highlight or underline these to review again in the future.

Definitions

[1] **Blasphemy** – Any speech, writing, or action that slanders God. In the OT, the penalty for blasphemy was death (Lev. 24:16).

[2] **Parable** – A story that uses everyday imagery and activities to communicate a spiritual truth. Jesus often taught in parables.

[3] **Demon** – An evil spirit that can inhabit ("possess") a human being and influence him or her to carry out its will. Demons were rebel angels, originally created by God, and they are always limited by God. Jesus and his followers cast out many demons, demonstrating the coming of the kingdom of God and Jesus' superiority. All demons will one day be destroyed along with Satan (Matt. 25:41; Rev. 20:10).

WEEK 5: JESUS' WORK BEYOND GALILEE

Mark 6:7–8:26

At this point in Mark, the systematically trained disciples are sent out to spread the message of God's kingdom, to heal, and to cast out demons. In Mark 6–8 Jesus again demonstrates his authority and warns his disciples against hard hearts. Also, the trickle of opposition against Jesus from the religious authorities begins to increase; it will turn into a flood of hostility in the second half of Mark.

The Big Picture

In Mark 6:7–8:26 Jesus sends out the twelve disciples, continues to manifest the coming kingdom through teaching and miracles, and begins to meet major opposition to his ministry.

> ## Reflection and Discussion

Read through the complete passage for this study, Mark 6:7–8:26. Then review the questions below and write your notes on them concerning this phase of Jesus' life and ministry. (For further background, see the *ESV Study Bible*, pages 1904–1910; also available online at www.esv.org.)

In Mark 6:7–13, Jesus sends out the twelve, as anticipated in Mark 3:14–15. What do we learn about the nature of their mission from the instructions they are given here in Mark 6? In light of the Old Testament, what significance might there be in sending out *twelve*? How might Exodus 12:11 inform the background to Jesus' instructions in Mark 6:8–9?

How does the death of John the Baptist in Mark 6:14–29 cast an ominous shadow on Jesus' future?

Mark says that Jesus saw the people "like sheep without a shepherd" (Mark 6:34). Read Genesis 48:15, Numbers 27:17, Psalm 23:1–4, and Isaiah 40:11, and notice what God promises in Jeremiah 23:2–4 and Ezekiel 34:10–16. What light might these Old Testament texts shed on who Jesus is and what he has come to do (note also John 10:11)? In light of Jeremiah 3:15, what might be the significance of Jesus' observation in Mark 6:34 combined with the fact that Jesus went on to *feed* these people?

In Mark 6:45–52 Jesus walks on the water. Comparing Mark's statement that Jesus "meant to *pass by*" the disciples (6:48) with Exodus 33:19, 22; 34:6, and Job 9:8, 11, what do we learn here about Jesus' identity?

In Mark 7:1–23 a conflict with the Pharisees[1] about hand-washing leads to a teaching by Jesus on moral defilement. What is the essence of Jesus' critique? How does he link up the mistake of the Pharisees with the mistake God's people have made in centuries past (note Mark 7:6–7)? What are ways we fall into the same error today?

Throughout Scripture, the "heart" refers to the center of one's being, including the mind, emotions, and will. When Jesus speaks of the heart in Mark 7:21, what is he saying about the fallen human condition? How does this differ from the way some Jews used the Old Testament ceremonial law to regulate their diet and state of "cleanliness" (cf. Mark 7:15)?

Jesus' response to the Syrophoenician woman is perplexing at first—how could Jesus withhold mercy from her, even calling her a dog (Mark 7:24–30)? Yet the special calling of Israel as God's own people is a whole-Bible theme, found not only in the Old Testament but also the New Testament (e.g., Rom. 1:16; 9:4–5). How does the woman's response indicate humility and persistence?

Unlike the feeding of the five thousand (Mark 6:30–44), which occurred in Galilee, the feeding of the four thousand in Mark 8:1–10 probably took place in Gentile[2] territory. Taken with Mark 7:24–30, what does the feeding of the 4,000 show about who Jesus is for Gentiles?

In Mark 8:11–21, the Pharisees again argue with Jesus, leading Jesus to expose his own disciples' failure to fully comprehend Jesus' identity and mission. The disciples perceive that Jesus is the Messiah, as Peter will announce later in Mark 8, but they do not yet perceive that he has come as a *suffering* Messiah. How might the two-staged healing of the blind man (Mark 8:22–26) demonstrate this partial understanding—especially in the way it is placed between Jesus' diagnosis of his disciples' slow understanding, on the one hand (8:14–21), and Peter's confession of Jesus as the Messiah, on the other (8:27–30)?

Read through the following three sections on *Gospel Glimpses*, *Whole-Bible Connections*, and *Theological Soundings*. Then take time to reflect on the *Personal Implications* these sections may have for your walk with the Lord.

Gospel Glimpses

RELENTLESS COMPASSION. Upon returning from their apostolic ministry, the twelve disciples are exhausted. "Come away … and rest a while," says Jesus (Mark 6:31). Jesus too, doubtless, was tired. Yet upon seeing the crowd, "he had compassion on them" (6:34). This is the heart of Jesus. Indeed, the one place in all four Gospel accounts where Jesus tells us about his *heart* is Matthew 11:29: "I am gentle and lowly in heart." Burrow in to the very core of what makes Jesus tick, and this is it. Gentleness. Compassion. Since Jesus is the exact representation of God, this ought not to surprise us, for this is what God himself is (Ex. 34:6–7).

THE HEART OF THE MATTER. In Mark 7:14–23 Jesus turned upside down the long-held Jewish view of clean and unclean food. Explaining that it is what comes out of a person that defiles, not what goes into him, Jesus "declared all foods clean" (7:19). Here we see Jesus continuing to strip away any sense of externally leveraged behavior management as determining our cleanliness before God. What matters is the heart.

BRINGING NOTHING BUT OUR NEED. The Syrophoenician woman, at first glance, could not have been a more unlikely candidate for receiving blessing from Jesus. She is a foreigner, a woman, and the mother of a child possessed by a demon (Mark 7:24–30). Yet she receives attention and help from Jesus without bringing any self-generated contribution on her part. She brings no moral resume, no lawkeeping, no impressiveness. All she brings is her need. She simply believed, humbly and persistently, that even the crumbs of mercy from Jesus would provide the help she so desperately needed.

Whole-Bible Connections

THE SENDING OUT OF THE TWELVE. God selected the twelve sons of Jacob to be his chosen people. These twelve sons were the fathers of the twelve tribes of Israel. They were to be a blessing to the whole world (Gen. 12:1–3) and God's special chosen people (Ex. 19:5–6). The Old Testament recounts the consistent failure, however, of the twelve tribes to do this—indeed, the tribes were hardly able to get along with one another! In the New Testament, God in Christ once more calls out twelve men, whose task it is, once again, to bring God's blessing to the world (Mark 6:7–13; note Rev. 21:9–17). The twelve apostles were thus called to carry on the work God had begun way back in the calling of Abraham, Isaac, and Jacob.

THE GOOD SHEPHERD. "God ... has been my shepherd all my life long," said Jacob (Gen. 48:15). "The LORD is my shepherd," wrote David (Ps. 23:1). God "will tend his flock like a shepherd," prophesied Isaiah (Isa. 40:11). Over time, these ancient descriptions of God as the true shepherd fueled the longing for a shepherd-leader, a shepherd-king, a Messiah, who would lead God's sheep in wisdom and restoration—"But you, O Bethlehem Ephrathah, who are too little to be among the clans of Judah, from you shall come forth for me one who is to be ruler in Israel, whose coming forth is from of old, from ancient days. ... And he shall stand and shepherd his flock in the strength of the LORD" (Mic. 5:2, 4; note also Num. 27:16–17; Jer. 3:15; 23:4). In the feeding of the five thousand, and especially in Mark 6:34, we see Jesus fulfilling this ancient longing and promise (see also John 10:11).

CLEAN AND UNCLEAN. The first act of rebellion the world had ever known had to do with putting something in the mouth and eating it (Gen. 3:6). We have been twisting God's gift of food ever since. The food laws in the Mosaic law provided one opportunity to do this. Some first-century Pharisees had made these laws primary as the way of regulating their ceremonial "cleanliness" (Mark 7:1–23). Jesus, however, "declared all foods clean" (Mark 7:19), uprooting the overscrupulous dietary regulation that had come to overshadow more important issues of the heart, where true cleanliness is determined—and which was the point of the law all along.

Theological Soundings

SUFFERING AND DIVINE SOVEREIGNTY. Mark 6:14–29 recounts the discouraging events leading up to the death of John the Baptist. John had faithfully heralded the coming of Jesus, not seeking glory for himself (John 3:30). Refusing to please men rather than God, John had spoken out against the marriage of Herod Antipas to Herodias, the wife of his brother, Herod Philip (Mark 6:18). Imprisoned for this, John was executed at the request of Herodias's daughter, who had danced before the royal court and pleased Herod so much that he offered her up to half his kingdom—upon which she requested the head of John the Baptist. We see here that the Lord's mysterious providence does not allow us to draw straight lines from personal faithfulness to earthly comfort. As the writer to the Hebrews makes clear, faith can lead to both triumph (Heb. 11:32–34) and suffering (Heb. 11:35–38).

SIN. "What comes out of a person is what defiles him. For from within, out of the heart of man, come evil thoughts, sexual immorality, theft, murder, adultery, coveting, wickedness, deceit, sensuality, envy, slander, pride, foolishness. All these evil things come from within, and they defile a person" (Mark 7:20–23). Jesus clarifies here our understanding of the fallen human condition. It is not what goes into us, but what comes out of us, that is defiling. The human condition is not one of cleanness in danger of defilement. Rather, our condition is one of defilement—manifested by what comes out of us—and is thus in need of cleansing.

Personal Implications

Take time to reflect on the implications of Mark 6:7–8:26 for your own life today. Make notes below on the personal implications for your walk with the Lord of (1) the *Gospel Glimpses*, (2) the *Whole-Bible Connections*, (3) the *Theological Soundings*, and (4) this passage as a whole.

1. Gospel Glimpses

2. Whole-Bible Connections

3. Theological Soundings

4. Mark 6:7–8:26

Take a moment now to ask for the Lord's blessing and help as you continue in this study of Mark. And take a moment also to look back through this unit of study, to reflect on a few key things that the Lord may be teaching you—and perhaps to highlight or underline these to review again in the future.

Definitions

[1] **Pharisee** – A member of a popular religious party in NT times characterized by strict adherence to the law of Moses and also to extrabiblical Jewish traditions. The Pharisees were frequently criticized by Jesus for their hypocritical practices. The apostle Paul was a zealous Pharisee prior to his conversion.

[2] **Gentile** – Anyone who is not Jewish. At times the NT uses the term "Greek" as a synonym for Gentile (e.g., 1 Cor. 1:22–23).

Week 6: True Discipleship and Transfiguration

Mark 8:27–9:50

▲

The Place of the Passage

This is the pinnacle and hinge of Mark's Gospel. Immediately following Peter's confession of Jesus as the Messiah in Mark 8:29, the whole Gospel swivels around and begins moving in a different direction. After eight chapters of accumulating amazement at Jesus by the crowds and the disciples (with occasional opposition from the Jewish authorities), Jesus suddenly begins to foretell his coming suffering and death. Halfway through Mark, the disciples have been decisively convinced that Jesus is the Messiah for whom they have been waiting. Now they learn that he will be a suffering Messiah.

The Big Picture

In Mark 8:27–9:50 Jesus begins to predict the suffering and death, followed by resurrection, that awaits him, explaining that such humiliation-followed-by-exaltation is the lot of all who follow him.

▶ Reflection and Discussion

Read through the complete passage for this study, Mark 8:27–9:50. Then review the questions below and write your notes on them concerning this phase of Jesus' life and ministry. (For further background, see the *ESV Study Bible*, pages 1910–1913; also available online at www.esv.org.)

In Mark 8:27–30 Peter speaks for the Twelve and confesses Jesus as the Christ, i.e., the divinely appointed leader and Messiah (2 Sam. 7:14–16; Psalm 2; Jer. 23:5–6) whom they expect to liberate the Jewish people from the oppressive yoke of Rome (see John 6:15). Peter's confession is God-given (note Matt. 16:17) but incomplete. How is it incomplete? In light of what Jesus goes on to say in Mark 8:31, what did Peter and the disciples not yet grasp about Jesus? How might this illumine Jesus' order in Mark 8:30?

Up until chapter 8, we have not seen any predictions of future suffering for Jesus. Instead, we observe:

- "his fame spread everywhere" (1:28)
- "they were all amazed" (2:12)
- "everyone marveled" (5:20)
- onlookers "were immediately overcome with amazement" (5:42)
- the disciples "were utterly astounded" (6:51)
- the crowds "were astonished beyond measure" (7:37)

Scan through Mark 8–10 and notice, by way of contrast, every time Jesus predicts his suffering and death.

Read Daniel 7:9–14, noting especially verse 13. This is the text that Jesus appears to have had in mind more than any other in referring to himself as the "Son of Man" (Mark 8:31). How does the depiction of the "son of man" in Daniel 7 make even more surprising Jesus' prediction of his imminent suffering in Mark 8:31?

Upon a careful reading of Mark 8:34–38, what is the reason for self-denial on the part of a disciple of Jesus? What is the danger if we resist self-denial and instead pursue the things of the world? How has Jesus set a pattern for self-denial in his own life in the verses immediately before Mark 8:34?

Jesus' statement in Mark 9:1 is puzzling. Is he implying that some of the people living at that time would see Christ's second coming[1]? Was Jesus mistaken about the timing of his return? No. Read 2 Peter 1:16–18, and consider the event that immediately follows Jesus' statement in Mark 9:1, in reflecting on what Jesus might have been referring to in speaking of "some" of his disciples seeing "the kingdom of God . . . come with power."

Jesus' transfiguration[2] (Mark 9:2–13) affords a glimpse into the radiant and divine glory of Jesus (Heb. 1:3), who is God's Son and Lord of all. What is the biblical significance of Jesus becoming "radiant, intensely white"(Mark 9:3), in light of Dan. 7:9; Luke 24:4; Acts 1:10; Rev. 20:11?

Moses represents the Law[3] (see Ex. 24:1, 9) and Elijah represents the Prophets[4] (see 1 Kings 19:8). What is the significance of these two men from Israel's past appearing with Jesus in Mark 9:4? Note Matt. 5:17 in considering your answer.

Mark 9:14–29 recounts an episode of a demon-possessed boy whom the disciples seek to liberate but cannot. What does this passage indicate about the key failure on the part of the crowd and the disciples? Note especially verses 19 and 23. How does the father of the boy represent what the disciples lacked, even if not perfectly (v. 24)?

Jesus turns upside down his disciples' intuitive understanding of what defines true greatness in Mark 9:33–37. How does he do this? How does the broader story told in Mark's Gospel portray Jesus as supremely displaying the kind of service and humility he commends in Mark 9:33–37?

At first glance Jesus' statement in Mark 9:40—"the one who is not against us is for us"—seems to contradict Jesus' statement in Matthew 12:30—"Whoever is not with me is against me." How do these two statements cohere? In considering an answer note closely just who is being described in each verse. Observe the key phrase that is repeated in both Mark 9:38 and 9:39; likewise consider the context, and who is being described, in Matthew 12:22–32.

In the final section of Mark 9 Jesus teaches about sin and temptation. He has already emphasized that receiving lowly persons in Christ's name means receiving him (v. 37); now he warns against causing such people "who believe in me to sin" (9:42). This leads to an extended teaching on sin and the measures that must be taken to avoid it (9:43–48). What is the central point Jesus is making in vv. 43–48? Does he mean that we should literally cut off parts of our bodies if they are causing us to sin? In answering, consider the nature of sin as described in Mark 7:20–23.

Read through the following three sections on *Gospel Glimpses*, *Whole-Bible Connections*, and *Theological Soundings*. Then take time to reflect on the *Personal Implications* this passage from Mark may have for your walk with the Lord.

Gospel Glimpses

REJECTED ON OUR BEHALF. Three times in this portion of Mark, Jesus speaks of his impending suffering (8:31; 9:12, 31). Here we are given a glimpse into the very heart of the whole Bible. Jesus says that he is going to be rejected by the religious authorities of the day, and that is of course true. But at a deeper level, on the cross Jesus felt himself rejected by his own Father (Mark 15:34; Rom. 8:32). Jesus experienced rejection not only horizontally, by men, but also vertically, by God. Jesus felt the full force of ultimate rejection, a rejection that you and I deserve but which, in Christ, we will never experience.

THE LAST AND THE FIRST. "If anyone would be first, he must be last of all and servant of all" (Mark 9:35). With these words Jesus gave his disciples the secret key to true greatness. But this truth—service leading to true greatness, the last winding up first—is embodied most clearly in Jesus himself. Jesus Christ is the only person ever to walk this earth who truly deserved to be first, to be great, but on the cross he made himself last, servant of all, so that you and I, who deserve to be last, can be treated as first.

Whole-Bible Connections

SON OF MAN. Five times in Mark 8:27–9:50 Jesus refers to himself as the "Son of Man" (8:31, 38; 9:9, 12, 31). Though this title assumes Jesus' humanity, its main significance lies in its hearkening back to Daniel 7. Here Daniel has a vision of "one like a son of man" being presented to "the Ancient of Days," God (Dan. 7:13). This son of man is no mere mortal—he comes on the clouds of heaven, and is given authority and glory and an everlasting kingdom (Dan. 7:13–14). This son of man, then, is a kingly figure. This fact likely connects this title with the "son of David" who will also, according to 2 Sam. 7:12–16, reign forever (and note Bartimaeus's crying out to Jesus as the son of David in 10:47–48). Jesus is this coming king.

THE CLOUD OF GLORY. During the course of Jesus' transfiguration, as he stood with Moses and Elijah, "a cloud overshadowed them, and a voice came out of the cloud" (Mark 9:7). Why a cloud? The coming of a cloud, and its representing the presence and glory of God, shows up at important points throughout the Bible, especially in the book of Exodus. The Lord leads his people by a pillar of cloud (Ex. 13:21–22), speaks to his people by appearing in a cloud (Ex. 16:9–10), gives his people the Ten Commandments amid a cloud (Ex. 19:9, 16; 24:15–18), descends in a cloud when Moses enters the tent to speak with him (Ex. 33:9; 40:34–38), and proclaims his name in a cloud (Ex. 34:5). Throughout the Bible the cloud signifies God's glory-filled presence, and in the transfiguration Jesus appears below a cloud because he is the climactic display of the glory of God (cf. John 1:14). Jesus and the cloud are then explicitly brought together in the final judgment at the end of the Bible in John's vision of "a white cloud, and seated on the cloud one like a son of man" (Rev. 14:14).

Theological Soundings

SATAN AND DEMONS. "Get behind me, Satan!" says Jesus (Mark 8:33). To whom is Jesus speaking? Peter—but Jesus addresses Peter as Satan. It was not Peter personally that Jesus was rejecting as satanic. Rather it was Peter's mind-set and worldly thinking, thinking that rejected suffering as a viable path for the Messiah. We learn here the insidious nature of the forces of evil: even Peter, one of the disciples closest to Jesus, was capable of falling into patterns of thinking that aligned with Satan rather than God. On the other hand, in Mark 9 the disciples are concerned that strangers are casting out demons in Jesus' name (9:38). Mark 8, then, shows us that the work of Satan can be done by those close to Jesus; Mark 9 shows us that the work of God can still be done by those far from Jesus.

HELL. In the course of teaching on temptation, Jesus calls hell "the unquench-able fire" (Mark 9:43) and the place "where their worm does not die and the fire is not quenched" (9:48). Jesus had already spoken in Mark 8:35–36 of losing one's life and forfeiting one's soul. While the language chosen here is metaphorical, the horror of what is being depicted is not. Hell is a real place, reserved for those who refuse to repent and trust Christ. According to Jesus, hell is a place of "unquenchable" torment, a fire that "is not quenched." Though it is difficult to swallow and almost too horrible to think about, the awful real-ity awaiting those who reject God's free offer of salvation is eternal, unending torment under the wrath of God.

Personal Implications

Take time to reflect on the implications of Mark 8:27–9:50 for your own life today. Make notes below on the personal implications for your walk with the Lord of (1) the *Gospel Glimpses*, (2) the *Whole-Bible Connections*, (3) the *Theological Soundings*, and (4) this passage as a whole.

1. Gospel Glimpses

2. Whole-Bible Connections

3. Theological Soundings

4. Mark 8:27–9:50

> ## As You Finish This Unit . . .

Take a moment now to ask for the Lord's blessing and help as you continue in this study of Mark. And take a moment also to look back through this unit of study, to reflect on a few key things that the Lord may be teaching you—and perhaps to highlight or underline these to review again in the future.

Definitions

[1] **Christ's second coming** – The OT looked forward to the coming of the Messiah, the Christ. Surprisingly, when the Christ came and the kingdom of God dawned, this new age brought forgiveness of sins yet did not bring full redemption of the body and the physical world. Sin and suffering remained. Thus the Christ has already come once, decisively inaugurating the new world longed for in the OT, and the Christ will come again, bringing to full and final fulfillment the redemption of the cosmos and the eradication of all sin and suffering.

[2] **Transfiguration** – An event in the life of Jesus Christ in which his physical appearance was transfigured, that is, changed to reflect his heavenly glory.

[3] **Law** – When spelled with an initial capital letter, "Law" refers to the first five books of the Bible. The Law contains numerous commands of God to his people, including the Ten Commandments and instructions regarding worship, sacrifice, and life in Israel. The NT often uses "the law" (lower case) to refer to the entire body of precepts set forth in the books of the Law, and reinforced by the rest of the Bible.

[4] **Prophet** – Someone who speaks authoritatively for God. When the NT refers to "the prophets," it is referring either to a specific group of OT books (e.g., Matt. 5:17; Luke 24:44), or, more generally, to those who spoke to God's people on behalf of God throughout the OT between the time of Moses and the close of the OT.

WEEK 7: INSTRUCTION ON DISCIPLESHIP

Mark 10:1–52

The Place of this Passage

We have seen that Mark 8 is the pinnacle and hinge of Mark. Here the Gospel's first eight chapters, and their portrayal of Jesus' attractive and well-received messianic identity, ends abruptly and a series of predictions of this Messiah's suffering and death begins (8:31–33; 9:30–32; 10:32–34; cf. 9:12). The unique contribution of chapter 10 to Mark's Gospel as a whole is the way in which it shows how Jesus connects his own path to that of his followers, turning upside down our expectations of what it means to be his disciple.

The Big Picture

Mark 10 shows us that the path of Christian discipleship is glory through suffering, as was the path of Jesus.

> ## Reflection and Discussion

In Mark 10 we see Jesus upending our intuitive assumptions about discipleship in four areas in particular: marriage, entrance into the kingdom, the Messiah's role, and personal significance. Read Mark 10:1–52 and consider the following questions. (For further background, see the *ESV Study Bible*, pages 1914–1917; also available online at www.esv.org.)

1. Upending Our Assumptions about Marriage and Divorce (10:1–12).

Once again, the Pharisees try to test Jesus and catch him (cf. 8:11; 12:15) with a question, this time concerning the legality of divorce. In essence, they are asking what grounds for divorce can be legitimately acted upon while remaining in God's good favor. How does Jesus respond?

What do we learn about the nature of marriage in Jesus' response?

2. Upending Our Assumptions about Entering the Kingdom (10:13–31).

Verses 13–16 set forth children as examples of the basic attitude everyone must have before he or she enters the kingdom of God (see also 9:35–36). In verse 24, talking to his disciples as the rich young man walks away, Jesus once again speaks of "children" and entering "the kingdom of God." Mark is setting up a deliberate contrast between empty-handed reception of the kingdom "like a child," on the one hand, and the attitudes of the rich young man and Peter and the disciples, on the other. What might it look like to "receive the kingdom of God like a child" (v. 15)?

In answering the rich young man's earnest inquiry about what must be done to enter the kingdom, Jesus holds out before him the "horizontal" commands of the Ten Commandments,[1] those having to do with human relationships ("do not defraud" probably combines the eighth and ninth commandments). While these have all been kept by the young man, Jesus has left off the "vertical" commands—most notably the first, "You shall have no other gods before me" (Ex. 20:3). Why might Jesus have done this?

In Jewish culture in biblical times, wealth was viewed as a sign of God's favor and blessing—it was a given that "the blessing of the LORD makes rich" (Prov. 10:22; see also 1 Kings 3:10–13; Job 42:12; Prov. 8:18; 10:4, 15; 14:24; 22:4; Eccles. 5:19). How does this help make sense of the disciples' astonishment (Mark 10:24, 26) at Jesus' statements regarding the difficulty of the rich entering the kingdom of God (vv. 23, 24–25)?

3. Upending Our Assumptions about the Messiah's Role (10:32–34).

For the third time in as many chapters, Jesus tells the disciples of his impending death and resurrection.[2] Hearing it, the disciples "were amazed" (cf. v. 24). Why? What assumption is Jesus here upending? In answering, consider the kind of messiah expected by the Jews in New Testament times.

Each of Jesus' major predictions of his death and resurrection (8:31; 9:30–32; 10:32–34) is followed by instruction in discipleship (8:32–38; 9:35–37; 10:35–45). Here in 10:32, Mark makes a point of telling us that "Jesus was walking ahead of them" in the march to Jerusalem and the cross. What does all this reveal about the connection between the path walked by Jesus and the path to be walked by his disciples?

----

4. Upending Our Assumptions about Personal Significance (10:35–52).

James and John rightly understand that Jesus is the long-awaited Messiah, the son of David, who will one day sit on the throne in everlasting rule (see 2 Sam. 7:1–17, esp. vv. 12–16). But they continue to understand Jesus' messianic rule only in terms of the first half of Mark's Gospel. They have not fully grasped ("You do not know what you are asking," Mark 10:38) that the road to the throne for Jesus lies directly through suffering, the very suffering Jesus has just been explaining to them in verses 32–34, as throughout Mark 8–10. What is the response of the rest of the disciples when they learn of the request of James and John? What does this suggest to us about what was motivating James and John in their request?

_____

_____

_____

_____

_____

_____

Stepping back and viewing verses 35–52 as a whole, we find that Mark is again (as in vv. 13–31) contrasting two encounters. Notice the parallels between the two accounts—James and John on the one hand, blind Bartimaeus on the other. In both cases: (1) Jesus is confronted with an unfocused request for compassionate action (vv. 35, 48–50); (2) Jesus initially responds by asking "What do you want me to do for you?" (vv. 36, 51); and (3) the person or people making the request clearly understand that Jesus is the Messiah (vv. 37, 47–48). Yet James and John make a radically different request than does Bartimaeus. How so?

_____

_____

_____

_____

_____

_____

_____

Read through the following three sections on *Gospel Glimpses*, *Whole-Bible Connections*, and *Theological Soundings*. Then take time to reflect on the *Personal Implications* these sections may have for your walk with the Lord.

▶ Gospel Glimpses

UPSIDE-DOWN QUALIFICATION. A thread running through Mark 10 is the strange way in which people qualify for entrance into God's kingdom: namely, by sheer awareness of their inadequacy, nothing more. Thus little children possess all the qualification required, as they have not yet allowed a lifetime of idolatry to build up around their hearts, as the rich young man had. Peter and the disciples seemed to be in much better shape than the rich young man, for they had sacrificed everything the rich young man had refused to sacrifice; yet Mark compares the rich young man with Peter to show that both, in their own way, failed to grasp the grace of the kingdom. The young man thought keeping the commandments was the key to entering the kingdom, while Peter thought sacrifice was the key. Both considered themselves "first." But Jesus says, the "first will be last, and the last first" (v. 31).

TRUE VISION. We see the gospel of grace in the subtle contrast of James and John with blind Bartimaeus. To both parties Jesus asks, "What do you want me to do for you?" (vv. 36, 51), yet while James and John request glory, Bartimaeus requests mercy. James and John, though physically seeing, were spiritually blind; Bartimaeus, though physically blind, was spiritually seeing. It is those who know their need, not those who assume their superiority, on whom God pours out mercy. All we bring is an awareness of our need for that mercy.

▶ Whole-Bible Connections

THE MARRIAGE RELATIONSHIP. In answering the Pharisees' testing question about divorce, Jesus goes all the way back to the beginning to establish the foundation for marriage. While the Pharisees reach back to Deuteronomy 24 to ask about the Mosaic law's allowance for a certificate of divorce, Jesus reaches back even further, to Genesis. Marriage between one man and one woman, in permanent mutual faithfulness, was built into the fabric of the world from the start. And such faithful marriage is meant to provide a glimpse of the greatest romance of all, God's love for his own bride (Hosea 2; Eph. 5:32; Rev. 21:2).

VISION/BLINDNESS. A theme that appears throughout the Bible is that of spiritual vision versus spiritual blindness. This whole-Bible motif first shows up in Genesis 3, as Adam and Eve take of the forbidden fruit and "the eyes of both were opened" to experience what sin, guilt, and shame really are (Gen. 3:7), and the motif runs right through the Bible to the end of Revelation, where the new Jerusalem is described as requiring no created light by which to see, "for the glory of God gives it light, and its lamp is the Lamb" (Rev. 21:23). A prominent instance of the vision/blindness theme is Isa. 6:9–10, picked up by Jesus (Matt. 13:14–15), John (John 12:39–40), and Paul (Acts 28:25–27) to explain rejection of God's gracious salvation as blindness. Paul underscores this in 2 Corinthians 4, describing the light of creation as an analogy to the light that scatters the darkness of blind unbelief in the human heart. The motif of seeing/blindness is particularly meaningful to John, who uses it repeatedly throughout his Gospel and letters (e.g., John 3:3, 36; 6:30; 8:56; 9:1–41; 10:21; 11:37; 12:40; 14:19; 16:16–19; 1 John 2:11; 3:2). Ultimately, Jesus is "the light of the world" (John 8:12; 9:5; cf. 12:46).

Theological Soundings

IDOLATRY. The root issue in the account of the rich young man is not financial but, more deeply, spiritual. Though he dutifully kept most of the commandments, he had neglected the first commandment—the prohibition of idolatry. His real god was his wealth, as proven in his inability to follow Jesus if it meant parting with his possessions.

ATONEMENT. Jesus says in 10:45 that he came "to give his life as a ransom for many." The metaphor here is profound and gets at the heart of the whole Bible. Jesus views his people as held captive and in need of a "ransom," a payment to liberate them. Our profound debt is our sin, in which we are held captive, helpless unless someone helps us from the outside. Jesus himself settles this debt with the payment to the Father of his own blood on the cross as our substitute.

HEAVEN. The afterlife is mentioned twice in Mark 10. First, in verse 30 Jesus concludes his response to Peter's self-alleged sacrifice by commenting on the gift of eternal life "in the age to come." Jesus' point in context is that, along with the blessings of this life, eternal life in the coming age far outweighs any sacrifice made along the way (cf. Rom. 8:18; 2 Cor. 4:17–18; on "the age to come" see also Eph. 1:21; Heb. 6:5). Second, Jesus speaks of heaven to James and John, commenting that the seating at Jesus' right and left is not his to grant, "but it is for those for whom it has been prepared" (Mark 10:40). In Mark 10, then, we find affirmations of the supreme value of heaven as well as of the absolute divine prerogative as to who will enjoy it.

Personal Implications

Take time to reflect on the implications of Mark 10:1–52 for your own life today. Make notes below on the personal implications for your walk with the Lord of (1) the *Gospel Glimpses*, (2) the *Whole-Bible Connections*, (3) the *Theological Soundings*, and (4) this passage as a whole.

1. Gospel Glimpses

2. Whole-Bible Connections

3. Theological Soundings

4. Mark 10:1–52

As You Finish This Unit . . .

Take a moment now to ask for the Lord's blessing and help as you continue in this study of Mark. And take a moment also to look back through this unit of study, to reflect on a few key things that the Lord may be teaching you—and perhaps to highlight or underline these to review again in the future.

Definitions

[1] **Ten Commandments** – Also called the "ten words," these are the commands God gave to Moses on two stone tablets on Mount Sinai. Moses then brought these down to the people of Israel. These commandments were given to God's people after God redeemed them from Egyptian slavery, setting a pattern found throughout the Bible—God first shows mercy to his people, then calls them to live before him in integrity. Grace fuels obedience.

[2] **Resurrection** – The impartation of restored life to a dead person. The NT teaches that Christians have already been resurrected spiritually (Eph. 2:5–6; Col. 3:1), but they have not yet been raised physically (2 Cor. 5:1–5). Physical resurrection will happen at the end of time, when both the righteous and the wicked will be resurrected, the former to eternal life and the latter to retributive judgment (John 5:29).

Week 8: Entering and Judging Jerusalem

Mark 11:1–12:44

As chapter 11 opens, the Gospel of Mark begins hurtling toward its climactic conclusion in the cross of Christ. John the Baptist is dead, having prepared the way for Jesus. Jesus has gathered a following, including twelve disciples, who have been sent out and have returned. Jesus has announced his imminent suffering and death. And now the end has drawn near. As Jesus comes into Jerusalem, the opposition of the religious authorities heightens and Jesus presses home to his disciples some final lessons before going to the cross.

The Big Picture

In Mark 11:1–12:44 Jesus enters Jerusalem triumphantly, cleanses the temple, and authoritatively teaches both opponents and disciples.

Reflection and Discussion

Read through the complete passage for this study, Mark 11:1–12:44. Then review the questions below and write your notes on them concerning this phase of Jesus' life and ministry. (For further background, see the *ESV Study Bible*, pages 1917– 1922; also available online at www.esv.org.)

Read Psalm 118:25–26, Isaiah 9:1–7, Jeremiah 23:5–8, and Zechariah 9:9. What were these Old Testament writings looking forward to? How do these passages illuminate what is happening in Mark 11:1–11? (Note that "Save us, we pray" in Ps. 118:25 is the Hebrew expression that is transliterated into Greek as *hosanna*.)

In Mark 11 Jesus curses a barren fig tree (vv. 12–14), cleanses the temple[1] (vv. 15–19), and explains the cursing of the fig tree (vv. 20–25). The way Mark organizes his material in these passages (fig tree/temple cleansing/fig tree) suggests a connection between the cleansing of the temple and the cursing of the fig tree. What might that connection be? Read Jeremiah 8:13, Hosea 9:10, 16, and Joel 1:7 in considering your answer, and be sure to consider each Old Testament reference in light of its context.

"I tell you, whatever you ask in prayer, believe that you have received it, and it will be yours" (Mark 11:24). Some have mistakenly taken these words from Jesus to mean that as long as enough faith[2] is mustered up, God will answer any prayer request. But we must always have the same perspective that Jesus had— that is, confidence in God's power but also submission to his will (see Mark 14:36 for a prayer that even Jesus had turned down). How should we understand Jesus' words, then, in Mark 11:24? How might other biblical texts such as James 4:3 or 1 John 5:14 inform our understanding of what Jesus means?

What do the various elements of the parable that opens Mark 12 signify—the tenants, the vineyard, the servants, the son of the vineyard owner, and the vineyard owner? How do Old Testament passages such as Isaiah 5:1–7 shed light on this parable? How does this parable develop what has already been happening in Mark 11:12–25?

In Mark 12:13–37 we read of a series of questions that the religious authorities put to Jesus—a political question (12:13–17), a theological question (12:18–27), and a moral question (12:28–34). After these three questions Jesus turns the tables and asks them a question, a question about himself (12:35–37).

How does Jesus respond to the political questioning?

How does he respond to the theological questioning?

How does he respond to the moral questioning?

Follow Jesus' logic in his words about Psalm 110 in Mark 12:36. What doctrine does Jesus see this text affirming, and what is the reasoning he uses to get there?

In the final two accounts of Mark 12, Jesus contrasts two different kinds of piety. One kind is seen in 12:38–40 and the other is seen in 12:41–44. What is the difference between the two? What is Jesus teaching his disciples through these contrasting examples?

Read through the following three sections on *Gospel Glimpses, Whole-Bible Connections,* and *Theological Soundings*. Then take time to reflect on the *Personal Implications* this passage from Mark may have for your walk with the Lord.

Gospel Glimpses

FROM THE INSIDE OUT. "To love him with all the heart and with all the understanding and with all the strength, and to love one's neighbor as oneself, is much more than all whole burnt offerings and sacrifices" (Mark 12:33). With these words a scribe shows that he is, in Jesus' words, "not far from the kingdom of God" (12:34). This scribe understands that the true intent of the Law of Moses was to generate a culture of love: love to God and love to man. If the people of God lose that ultimate goal amid an elaborate system of sacrifices and offerings, they have missed the whole purpose of the law. It is the heart, not externally managed sacrifices, that is precious to God. This scribe understood that the good news of Jesus restores us from the inside out, not from the outside in.

NO PREREQUISITES REQUIRED. Followers of Jesus Christ are not required to qualify with any self-generated prerequisites. Indeed, self-conscious reflection on personal virtue can be positively detrimental. We see this in the back-to-back accounts of Jesus' warning about the scribes' glamour (Mark 12:38–40) and the widow's offering (12:41–44). The scribes were respected and admired. They knew the Scripture well. They had "the best seats in the synagogues" (12:39). And they, Jesus says, on account of their poor treatment of widows, "will receive the greater condemnation" (12:40). The widow, on the other hand, had nothing in herself to commend her to God, and she knew it. In God's sight, however, her tiny gift was greater than the showy generosity of "many rich people" (12:41). No ostentation. No parading. Just simple, quiet, sacrificial giving. Once more, God sees what man does not see.

Whole-Bible Connections

DAVID'S KINGDOM. "Hosanna!" the people shout as Jesus rides into Jerusalem. "Blessed is he who comes in the name of the Lord! Blessed is the coming kingdom of our father David!" (Mark 11:9–10). Way back in 2 Samuel 7, God had promised to David a kingdom that would never end (v. 16), and rest from all Israel's enemies (v. 11). When the people shout "Blessed is he who comes in the name of the Lord" at Jesus' entry, they are picking up on this promise to David as it is reiterated in Psalm 118:25–26, which is a prayer of blessing for the coming messianic kingdom. The people see Jesus' entrance into Jerusalem as the fulfillment of these ancient promises. Even more ancient than the echoes of the Davidic promise are the echoes of the exodus from Egypt: the Triumphal Entry takes place at the beginning of Passover week, which recalls the Jewish people's liberation from Egyptian slavery. Jesus is indeed the long-awaited son of David, the king, who leads his people to true freedom—freedom not from Rome but from sin and death.

TEMPLE. God first dwelt with his people in Eden. Here, uninterrupted, the divine and the human intersected. The eternal and the temporal met. Eden was, in other words, the first temple. When Adam and Eve fell, that fellowship was fractured, and in the centuries following, God's presence with his people was restricted to a tabernacle and then a man-made temple. When Jesus overturned the tables in the temple in Mark 11, he was reminding the people that the temple is not for financial transaction between people and other people, but for spiritual transaction between people and God. A few chapters later Jesus is crucified, "and the curtain of the temple was torn in two" (Mark 15:38), thus opening the way back into God's presence. Jesus hereby accomplished the purpose of the temple: he restored fellowship between people and God.

FRUITFUL TREES. Israel was called to be a fruitful tree but failed: "When I would gather them, declares the LORD, there are no grapes on the vine, nor figs on the fig tree; even the leaves are withered" (Jer. 8:13; see also Hos. 9:10, 16; Joel 1:7). When Jesus sandwiches his cleansing of the temple in between the two halves of the cursing of the barren fig tree, this symbolizes more than a hungry and frustrated Messiah. This cursing signifies judgment over Israel's fruitlessness (note also the parable that opens Mark 12, which describes Israel in terms of a "vineyard"). Jesus himself, however, went to the cross—was judged and treated as "fruitless"—so that fallen people like us can become the fruitful trees we were meant to be (John 15:1–8).

> ## Theological Soundings

RESURRECTION. The Sadducees, who reject the doctrine of a future bodily resurrection, try to catch Jesus in a theological trap. They ask which of seven brothers will have as his wife in heaven the one woman they were all legally married to at different times on earth. In responding, Jesus affirms the resurrection that is to come, saying that believers will then be "like angels in heaven" (Mark 12:25). The angels of heaven do not marry; neither will believers. Jesus seems to be saying that the existence experienced by those in the next life is on another plane than that of our present existence on earth. Marriage is left behind for the matchless experience of being in the presence of God. The bodily resurrection promised to believers will be similar to our current existence in some ways—Jesus, after all, is the "firstfruits" (1 Cor. 15:20), the first instance of the resurrected body all believers will one day have, and Jesus' resurrection body was thoroughly physical. Yet the next life will also be very different from life now (1 Cor. 15:40).

CHRISTOLOGY. The people have already declared that Jesus is the coming king, the Messiah, the long-anticipated son of David (Mark 11:10). In Mark 12, however, Jesus teaches that the Messiah is not only David's son but also, according to Psalm 110, David's Lord. How can the Messiah be both? Here Jesus is anticipating being exalted to the right hand of God as God's own Son. Jesus is not only the son of David, he is the Son of God—and thus he is included in the divine identity. The Messiah, Jesus is teaching, is no mere mortal.

Personal Implications

Take time to reflect on the implications of Mark 11:1–12:44 for your own life today. Make notes below on the personal implications for your walk with the Lord of (1) the *Gospel Glimpses*, (2) the *Whole-Bible Connections*, (3) the *Theological Soundings*, and (4) this passage as a whole.

1. Gospel Glimpses

2. Whole-Bible Connections

3. Theological Soundings

4. Mark 11:1–12:44

As You Finish This Unit . . .

Take a moment now to ask for the Lord's blessing and help as you continue in this study of Mark. And take a moment also to look back through this unit of study, to reflect on a few key things that the Lord may be teaching you—and perhaps to highlight or underline these to review again in the future.

Definitions

[1] **Temple** – A special building set aside as holy because of God's presence there. Solomon built the first temple of the Lord in Jerusalem, to replace the portable tabernacle. This temple was later destroyed by the Babylonians, rebuilt, and then destroyed again by the Romans. Jesus is the true and final temple (John 2:18–22), and all those united to him become part of this temple too (Eph. 2:20–22).

[2] **Faith** – Trust in or reliance upon something or someone for solid reasons, yielding certainty. Salvation, which is purely a work of God's grace, can be received only through faith in Jesus Christ (Rom. 5:2; Eph. 2:8–9). The writer of Hebrews calls on believers to emulate those who lived godly lives by faith (Hebrews 11).

WEEK 9: JESUS AND THE COMING JUDGMENT

Mark 13:1–37

▲

Jesus' public ministry is drawing to a close. He has made a final entrance into Jerusalem. He knows his death is imminent. Before eating the Passover one last time with his disciples and going to the cross, he teaches his disciples about events to come, both on the immediate horizon and in the distant future. His purpose is to focus the attention of the disciples on preparedness for troubles, on readiness to suffer, and on trust.

The Big Picture

Blending warning with comforting, Jesus prepares his disciples in Mark 13:1–37 for future hardships and temptations after he is gone.

> ### Reflection and Discussion

Read through the complete passage for this study, Mark 13:1–37. Then review the questions below and write your notes on them concerning this phase of Jesus' life and ministry. (For further background, see the *ESV Study Bible*, pages 1922–1926; also available online at www.esv.org.)

Herod the Great[1] had enlarged the second temple to about double the size of the temple Solomon had built, and the disciples marvel at the beauty of it in Mark 13:1. How does Jesus respond? Could it be that Jesus has more in mind than merely physical destruction of the temple? Bear in mind Mark 14:58 and 15:38 in considering your answer.

In response to Jesus' statement about the future destruction of the temple (13:2), the disciples ask him, "when will these things be, and what will be the sign when all these things are about to be accomplished?" Jesus' answer deals primarily with the second part of their question ("what will be the sign"), but he also addresses the timing of the coming events ("when"). Verses 5–23 focus on local and world events (destruction of the temple, persecution, and universal evangelism); vv. 24–27 focus on cosmic events (the transformation of the known cosmos and the coming of the Son of Man). The disciples assume that the destruction of the temple will coincide with the end of time, but Jesus corrects their thinking (vv. 7, 13).

As you glance over Mark 13:4–37, what do you think might be the central point Jesus wants to get across?

In Mark 13:9 –13, identify three hardships Jesus foretells and three comforts he provides as he encourages his disciples to be faithful witnesses to the nations.

The "abomination of desolation standing where he ought not to be" (v. 14) probably refers to Rome coming in AD 70 and destroying the temple—a place Gentiles were not to enter. In light of the importance of the temple to Mark, which we have traced throughout our study of this Gospel, reflect on the significance of the destruction of the temple. What would it mean to a first-century Jew?

The events described throughout vv. 14 –23 likely refer not only to the destruction of the temple but also, in an anticipatory way, to events more distant in the future having to do with the end of world history. What clues in the text lead us to this conclusion?

In Mark 13:24 –27 Jesus broadens his vision to focus on cosmic events in the more distant future than the tribulation[2] he has been describing in vv. 14 –23. Read Joel 2:10, 31 and Daniel 7:13, and consider the broader contexts (surrounding verses) of both of these Old Testament texts. How does Jesus refer to them, and what is the significance of such references?

Some have understood Jesus' illustration of the fig tree in Mark 13:28 as a symbol for the nation of Israel[3] (remember Mark 11:12–26). It is more likely, however, that in this case Jesus is just using a familiar event in nature as another illustration. What is the point of this illustration?

Jesus says that "this generation will not pass away until all these things take place" (Mark 13:30). This has perplexed interpreters, because it seems clear that at various points in Mark 13 Jesus has in mind the end of history, yet the "generation" to which Jesus refers would presumably have died out sometime in the first century. Perhaps by "this generation" Jesus has in mind "this evil generation" that will remain until Christ returns (cf. Matt. 12:45; Luke 11:29), or perhaps it refers to "this generation of believers" throughout the entire Christian age. Another option is that this is a prediction with multiple fulfillments. Whatever the precise meaning of Jesus' words, we know that his "words will not pass away" (Mark 13:31). Jesus is assuring his people of his wise oversight of human history, despite hardships for his followers.

Throughout Mark 13, Jesus emphasizes three things about future events. We can summarize them with three *i*'s: imminence, interval, and ignorance. Christ's final return is *imminent*—we must always be ready for it. Christ's return will come, however, after an *interval* of various events. And we are all *ignorant* of the precise time he will return. Where in Mark 13 do you see each of these three *i*'s?

Read through the following three sections on *Gospel Glimpses*, *Whole-Bible Connections*, and *Theological Soundings*. Then take time to reflect on the *Personal Implications* this passage from Mark may have for your walk with the Lord.

Gospel Glimpses

THE IRONIC REVERSAL. "They will deliver you over to councils, and you will be beaten in synagogues . . ." (Mark 13:9). The shock of this prediction by Jesus is that it is God's people, the Jews, the people of which Jesus was a part and to whom he came (John 1:11), who will persecute Jesus' disciples. The "councils" and "synagogues" are *Jewish* locales. Meanwhile, the gospel will "be proclaimed to all nations" (Mark 13:10). The insiders reject the gospel; the outsiders hear it and, as often in Mark's Gospel, receive it (e.g., Mark 7:24–30; 15:39). Such is the nature of the gospel. One reason for this is that it is those who know their need who will respond to the gospel; those who believe they are already "insiders" often fail to feel their need for the gospel.

CHOSEN IN GRACE. "But for the sake of the elect, whom he chose . . ." (Mark 13:20). Believers are those whom God chose. This does not mean we do not choose God. We do. But our choosing of him is rooted in his even deeper choosing of us (cf. 1 John 4:19). This divine choosing is solely on terms of grace. God does not choose those who "make the cut" in some way—morally, socially, intellectually. Instead, "God chose what is foolish in the world to shame the wise; God chose what is weak in the world to shame the strong" (1 Cor. 1:27).

Whole-Bible Connections

GOOD NEWS FOR GENTILES. Jesus says that "the gospel must ... be proclaimed to all nations" (Mark 13:10). On the one hand, the call to bring the gospel to the nations explodes in a new way in the New Testament. Think, for example, of Paul, the "apostle to the Gentiles" (Rom. 11:13; cf. Gal. 2:8; the same Greek word translated "Gentiles" here and elsewhere is used for "nations" in Mark 13:10). On the other hand, the call to bring the blessing of God to all peoples goes all the way back to the first book of the Bible. When God first called Abram, he declared that Abram would be a blessing to the other nations (Gen. 12:2–3). One of Israel's failures was the failure to bless the nations (see Jer. 4:1–2). At the end of all things, Mark 13:10 is fulfilled and "the nations walk" in the New Jerusalem and "the kings of the earth will bring their glory into it" (Rev. 21:24).

THE SUN AND THE MOON. In Genesis 1, God created "two great lights—the greater light to rule the day and the lesser light to rule the night" (Gen. 1:16). Throughout the Old Testament, the sun came to represent God's favor and blessing (Ps. 72:17; 84:11; 136:8). Judgment over godless nations was likewise described in terms of the sun and the moon ceasing to give light (Isa. 13:10; Ezek. 32:7). Due to Israel's repeated faithlessness, the prophets spoke of a coming day when even for Israel the sun would become dark (Joel 2:10, 30–31). Jesus picked up on this language in Mark 13, saying that in the tribulation "the sun will be darkened, and the moon will not give its light" (13:24). Judgment will come.

Theological Soundings

ESCHATOLOGY. The word *eschatology* means "last things" and refers to what Christians believe about the end times. From one perspective eschatology refers to the present, because the New Testament shows repeatedly that the ancient hopes and longings of the Old Testament have already decisively begun in Jesus and the church even if they are not yet fully completed. In considering eschatology as it surfaces in Mark 13, however, we are referring mainly to the end of history, when Jesus will come again. We learn in Mark 13 several important things about the second coming of Christ, including: (1) he will come "with great power and glory" (v. 26); (2) the elect (chosen) will be mercifully spared when Christ returns (vv. 20, 27); (3) there will be signs indicating that the end is near (vv. 28–29); (4) no one knows when Jesus will come (v. 32); and (5) believers must be vigilant and ready for Jesus to come at any time (vv. 33–36).

ELECTION. Three times in Mark 13 Jesus refers to "the elect," or "the chosen ones" (vv. 20, 22, 27). The Bible teaches that God is sovereign over all things, including the actions of human beings as moral agents, and yet moral agents are also responsible for their actions. God's sovereignty does not cancel out human responsibility, and human responsibility does not mitigate God's sovereignty. Both are true, even if our finite minds cannot fully comprehend how they fit together. One way the Bible underscores God's sovereignty is by speaking of believers, as Jesus does in Mark 13, as "the elect." They are called the elect because God has chosen ("elected") them to be his. This sovereign choice stretches back into time immemorial (Eph. 1:4). While God's sovereign will does not negate the need for true human repentance and faith, the Bible teaches that such repentance and faith are themselves the effect (not the cause) of God's providential working. Our salvation is a gift of grace from first to last.

▶ Personal Implications

Take time to reflect on the implications of Mark 13:1–37 for your own life today. Make notes below on the personal implications for your walk with the Lord of (1) the *Gospel Glimpses*, (2) the *Whole-Bible Connections*, (3) the *Theological Soundings*, and (4) this passage as a whole.

1. Gospel Glimpses

2. Whole-Bible Connections

3. Theological Soundings

4. Mark 13:1–37

As You Finish This Unit . . .

Take a moment now to ask for the Lord's blessing and help as you continue in this study of Mark. And take a moment also to look back through this unit of study, to reflect on a few key things that the Lord may be teaching you—and perhaps to highlight or underline these to review again in the future.

Definitions

[1] **Herod the Great** – Herod I, also known as Herod the Great, ruled Israel and Judah from 37–4 BC. He was not Roman by birth but had been appointed king of the Jews under the authority of Rome. He ruled firmly and at times ruthlessly, and was a master builder who not only restored the temple in Jerusalem but also built many theaters, cities, palaces, and fortresses.

[2] **Tribulation** – Trial or difficulty. In Christian theology regarding the end times, many believe the NT teaches that there will be a final, climactic, and intensified "tribulation" just prior to Christ's second coming.

[3] **Israel** – Originally, another name given to Jacob (Gen. 32:28). Later applied to the nation formed by his descendants, then to the ten northern tribes of that nation, who rejected the anointed king and formed their own nation. In the NT, the name is applied to the church as the spiritual descendants of Abraham (e.g., Gal. 6:16).

WEEK 10: JESUS' BETRAYAL AND TRIAL

Mark 14:1–15:15

▲

The Place of the Passage

This portion of Mark describes Jesus' last week, leading up to his crucifixion. As Jesus eats the Passover meal with his disciples, Judas has already agreed to betray Jesus, and Peter is on the verge of denying Jesus. The rapidly unfolding events of Mark 14–15 heighten the pace and tension of the Gospel of Mark as a whole, and the climactic death of Jesus is imminent.

The Big Picture

Mark 14:1–15:15 recounts the events of Jesus' final week, leading up to the cross—Passover with his disciples, betrayal by Judas, denial by Peter, and trial before the Jewish council.

▶ **Reflection and Discussion**

Read through the complete passage for this study, Mark 14:1–15:15. Then review the questions below and write your notes on them concerning this phase of Jesus' life and ministry. (For further background, see the *ESV Study Bible*, pages 1926–1930; also available online at www.esv.org.)

The opening verses to Mark 14 situate the narrative with respect to important Jewish events such as the Passover.[1] In light of the flow of Mark's Gospel, and what is ahead for Jesus, why might Mark want to alert the reader to these events? Consider 1 Corinthians 5:7.

A denarius was a day's wage for a worker, so when the woman (probably Mary the sister of Lazarus) in Mark 14:3–9 breaks an alabaster jar and pours over Jesus' head nard worth more than three hundred denarii, she is squandering almost a year's salary for a worker. Despite the protests of some who are there, Jesus does not object to what this woman has done. Why not?

At the Passover meal, the Jews remember and celebrate the beginning of Israel's deliverance from slavery, when the Lord brought judgment by killing the firstborn in every Egyptian house but "passed over" the Israelite houses where the blood of the Passover lamb had been applied (Ex. 12:7, 12–13, 22–28). Reflect on the theological significance of Jesus eating the Passover with his disciples at this point in Mark's Gospel.

What do we learn about the sovereignty[2] of God in Mark 14:21? See also Gen. 50:18–21, Acts 2:23, and Acts 4:27–28.

What does Jesus say the bread and the wine represent (Mark 14:22–25)? How do Old Testament texts such as Exodus 24:8, Isaiah 53:12, and Zechariah 9:11 shed light on this institution of the Lord's Supper[3] in Mark 14?

Read Zechariah 13:1–9. Although Jesus quotes only one verse from this passage (Zech. 13:7 in Mark 14:27), how does the whole passage in Zechariah shed light on broader events in Mark's Gospel?

Jesus has just shared the "cup" of the new covenant with his disciples in Mark 14:23–25. In the Garden of Gethsemane, Jesus then prays for the Father to take away this "cup" (14:36). The "cup" in Old Testament imagery represented God's wrath (Isa. 51:17–23; Jer. 25:15–18). What does this teach us about what Jesus is about to undergo?

Judas leads an armed crowd to Gethsemane and betrays Jesus with a kiss (Mark 14:43–45). Jesus is then led to the high priest (14:53), who asks Jesus, "Are you the Christ?" (14:61). Jesus responds with a theologically loaded answer that draws on various Old Testament texts: "I am, and you will see the Son of Man seated at the right hand of Power, and coming with the clouds of heaven" (14:62). Read Exodus 3:14, Psalm 110:1, and Daniel 7:13, along with their Old Testament contexts, to understand what Jesus is saying with this answer. How does the emphatic response of the high priest (Mark 14:63–64), who knew his Scripture well, clarify what Jesus is communicating?

How does Peter's denial of Jesus (Mark 14:66–72) advance the narrative of the final days of Jesus' life? That is, what do we learn about what Jesus suffered in these days?

In Mark 15:1–15 Jesus is led before "the whole council" (15:1), meaning the Jewish Sanhedrin.[4] It is here that Jesus is condemned to crucifixion under Pilate's jurisdiction. What ironies do you detect in Mark 15:1–15? Consider what Pilate asks Jesus (15:2), who it is who accuses Jesus (15:3), and whom Pilate releases (15:15).

Read through the following three sections on *Gospel Glimpses, Whole-Bible Connections,* and *Theological Soundings.* Then take time to reflect on the *Personal Implications* this passage from Mark may have for your walk with the Lord.

► Gospel Glimpses

AN UNANSWERED PRAYER. In the garden of Gethsemane Jesus prayed that, if possible, "the hour might pass from him" (Mark 14:35). "Remove this cup from me," he asked (14:36). As the remainder of Mark's Gospel goes on to show, however, this prayer was not granted. The hour did not pass from Jesus. The cup of God's wrath was not removed from him. While this is perplexing to read, it is also our great hope as believers. For it is because God turned down Jesus' prayer for deliverance that you and I can know that God will do whatever it takes to deliver us from sin and death. We can be assured that all our prayers are heard because Jesus had a prayer to which God said no. This is why we pray "in Jesus' name"—because his rejection on the cross means that believers can have free access to the Father.

ACCUSED IN OUR PLACE. Twice in Jesus' trial, once before the Jewish council (14:61) and once before Pilate (15:5), Jesus remained silent before his accusers—*false* accusers. This is a glorious glimpse into the great hope of the gospel. We who often feel the voice of accusation within do, in ourselves, deserve such condemnation. Jesus, however, heard the voice of accusation even though he did not deserve condemnation. Yet he underwent condemnation on the cross so that you and I, who unlike Jesus truly are guilty, can silence the voice of accusation that bubbles up within. For Jesus was accused and condemned on our behalf. As John Calvin said, "Jesus remained silent before Pilate so that ever after he might speak for us."

Whole-Bible Connections

THE PASSOVER LAMB. Mark 14 bristles with connections to the Passover event that is recorded in the book of Exodus. The Israelites celebrated Passover every year since their liberation from Egyptian captivity, a liberation that took place through the shed blood of a lamb. During the last of the ten plagues God sent on Egypt, in which God killed the firstborn of every Egyptian family, the angel of God "passed over" any Israelite houses that were marked with a lamb's blood. Picking up on this event, Jesus celebrated the Passover with his disciples in anticipation of the greatest liberation, in which another lamb was slain to save those who take refuge under its blood (see also 1 Pet. 1:19). Revelation picks up on this theme, exulting in those who have conquered "by the blood of the Lamb" (Rev. 12:11; note also 5:6; 7:14; 13:8; 22:1–3).

A GARDEN. The Bible opens with God's people in a garden containing a river and a fruit-bearing tree of life (Gen. 2:9–10) and closes with God's new people in a garden-city that likewise contains a river and a fruit-bearing tree of life (Rev. 22:1–2). Along the way, we see a hope for a restored garden in which God will once more dwell in happy fellowship with his people (Isa. 51:3; 58:11; Ezek. 36:35). How does the first garden, in which mankind plunged through sin into ruin and death, culminate in a restored garden, in which God's people enjoy restored fellowship with him? Only because at the pinnacle of all of human history, in another garden called Gethsemane, the last Adam (1 Cor. 15:45) was arrested and led off to be killed (Mark 14:32–50).

Theological Soundings

DIVINE SOVEREIGNTY. There are two ways we might err in understanding God's sovereignty. One way is to emphasize his sovereignty to the neglect of human responsibility. The other error is to so emphasize human responsibility that we neglect divine sovereignty. Mark 14:21 holds both together in a healthy tension: "For the Son of Man goes as it is written of him [divine sovereignty], but woe to that man by whom the Son of Man is betrayed [human responsibility]!" While Jesus' death was decreed long ago, this does not soften Judas's sin in betraying him; while Judas betrayed Jesus, this does not mean such betrayal surprised God or was contrary to God's wise providence.

THE LORD'S SUPPER. Protestant Christians acknowledge two sacraments instituted by the Lord Jesus Christ: baptism and the Lord's Supper. Baptism relates to entrance into the new covenant community, and the Lord's Supper relates to ongoing participation in that community. Specifically, the Lord's Supper is the church's way of regularly remembering and rejoicing in Jesus' sacrificial death on our behalf (Mark 14:22–25; also Matt. 26:26–29; Luke 22:18–20; 1 Cor. 11:23–26).

Personal Implications

Take time to reflect on the implications of Mark 14:1–15:15 for your own life today. Make notes below on the personal implications for your walk with the Lord of (1) the *Gospel Glimpses*, (2) the *Whole-Bible Connections*, (3) the *Theological Soundings*, and (4) this passage as a whole.

1. Gospel Glimpses

2. Whole-Bible Connections

3. Theological Soundings

4. Mark 14:1–15:15

As You Finish This Unit . . .

Take a moment now to ask for the Lord's blessing and help as you continue in this study of Mark. And take a moment also to look back through this unit of study, to reflect on a few key things that the Lord may be teaching you—and perhaps to highlight or underline these to review again in the future.

Definitions

[1] **Passover** – An annual Israelite festival commemorating God's final plague on the Egyptians, which led to the exodus. In this final plague, the Lord "passed over" the houses of those who spread the blood of a lamb on the doorposts of their homes (Exodus 12). Those who did not obey this command suffered the death of their firstborn. Jesus is the final and true Passover lamb (1 Cor. 5:7). See also "The Passover Lamb" under "*Whole-Bible Connections*" on page 80.

[2] **Sovereignty** – Supreme and independent power and authority. Sovereignty over all things is a distinctive attribute of God (1 Tim. 6:15–16). He directs all things to carry out his purposes (Rom. 8:28–29).

[3] **Lord's Supper** – A meal of remembrance instituted by Jesus on the night of his betrayal. Christians are to observe this meal, also called Communion, in remembrance of Jesus' death. It consists of wine, symbolizing the new covenant in his blood, and bread, symbolizing his body, which was broken for his followers. See also "The Lord's Supper" under "*Theological Soundings*" on pages 80–81.

[4] **Sanhedrin** – Either a local Jewish tribunal ("council," Matt. 5:22; "courts," Matt. 10:17) or as here, the supreme ecclesiastical court in Jerusalem (Matt. 26:59). These Jewish leaders included elders, chief priests, and scribes.

Week 11: Crucifixion and Resurrection

Mark 15:16–16:8

▲

The Place of the Passage

This passage is the climax of Mark. This is what the whole Gospel has been moving toward from the beginning. We have seen hints earlier in Mark that this Gospel account would climax in Jesus' death (e.g., Mark 10:45), and three times in the immediate wake of Peter's confession of Jesus as the Christ, Jesus predicted his imminent suffering (8:31; 9:31; 10:33–34). Now this suffering is upon him. But not only will he suffer and die, he will also rise again—as all three predictions also foretell.

The Big Picture

Mark 15:16–16:8 recounts the death, burial, and resurrection of Jesus Christ.

> **Reflection and Discussion**

Read through the complete passage for this study, Mark 15:16–16:8. Then review the questions below and write your notes on them concerning this phase of Jesus' life and ministry. (For further background, see the *ESV Study Bible*, pages 1931–1933; also available online at www.esv.org.)

The presence of "the whole battalion" (Mark 15:16), which at full strength would be about six hundred men, when Jesus is led away assumes that Jesus is a rebel against Rome. What are ways in which the Romans ridicule Jesus? Do you notice any irony in what they say to him in verse 18?

According to both Jewish and Roman custom, Jesus had to be taken outside the city walls to be crucified. What might be the theological significance of this, in light of other passages in the Bible such as Exodus 29:14, Leviticus 16:27, and Hebrews 13:11–12?

Crucifixion[1] was the final public deterrent to warn people not to rebel against Rome. In his crucifixion Jesus' hands were nailed below the wrist on the horizontal beam of the cross, and his feet were placed with one above the other and then nailed to the vertical beam. Consider the significance of the entire Old Testament sacrificial[2] system and reflect on the significance of what was happening when Jesus Christ was crucified.

Many Old Testament prophecies are fulfilled in the death of Jesus as recounted in Mark 15. Read Deuteronomy 21:23, Psalm 22, Isaiah 53, and Malachi 4:5–6, and jot down connections between these Old Testament passages and what takes place in Mark 15, especially in vv. 21–36.

As Jesus breathes his last, the Roman centurion standing nearby exclaims, "Truly this man was the Son of God!" (Mark 15:39). Aside from the words of demons (Mark 3:11; 5:7), there is only one other place in Mark where Jesus is called the Son of God. Read Mark 1:1. How might Mark 1:1 and 15:39 function in the Gospel of Mark as a whole?

What is the significance of the curtain of the temple being torn in two, from top to bottom, in Mark 15:38? Consider the role that the temple has played throughout the Gospel of Mark.

Along with Luke, Mark emphasizes the role of women in the final week of Jesus' life (Mark 15:40–41, 47; 16:1ff.). What might be the reason for this?

What details are given in Mark 15:42–47 to make clear that Jesus did indeed die? Why might Mark have wanted to make this clear?

On the third day, after the Jewish Sabbath, three women bring spices to anoint[3] Jesus (Mark 16:1). What do they see there? What is their reaction? How does Mark 16:6 fulfill numerous statements throughout the Gospel of Mark?

Note: Your Bible may have in brackets what is known as the "Longer Ending of Mark" (Mark 16:9–20). Some ancient manuscripts of Mark's Gospel contain these verses and others do not. This presents a puzzle for scholars who specialize in the history of such manuscripts. This longer ending is missing from various old and reliable Greek manuscripts, and early church fathers (such as Origen and Clement of Alexandria) did not appear to know of these verses. On the other hand, some early and many later manuscripts contain verses 9–20, and many church fathers (such as Irenaeus) evidently knew of them. As for the verses themselves, they contain various Greek words and expressions uncommon to Mark, and there are stylistic differences as well. Many think this shows verses 9–20 to be a later addition. In summary, verses 9–20 should be read with caution.

Read through the following three sections on *Gospel Glimpses*, *Whole-Bible Connections*, and *Theological Soundings*. Then take time to reflect on the *Personal Implications* this passage from Mark may have for your walk with the Lord.

Gospel Glimpses

REFUSING TO SAVE HIMSELF. The mocking religious authorities taunted Jesus, saying, "He saved others; he cannot save himself" (Mark 15:31). The deep irony of this is that it was by refusing to save himself that he did save others. Jesus could have called an army of angels to his side (Matt. 26:53). But he did not. He allowed himself to be condemned so that others could be saved. This is the glory of what Martin Luther called "the great exchange." Jesus took our condemnation on himself and gives us his righteousness as we look to him in faith.

GOD-FORSAKEN. "My God, my God, why have you forsaken me?" (Mark 15:34). The horror of the cross of Christ was not mainly its physical torture. The physical agony was truly horrific, but the greatest pain Christ underwent was his sense of divine abandonment. Jesus, echoing Psalm 22:1, does not call God "Abba," Father, in this moment, but "My God." Jesus was experiencing the full fury of the wrath of God—in our place. For believers, the judgment Jesus experienced on the cross is the judgment they deserve; it is what they would have experienced in the final judgment had they not repented and believed. When Jesus laments being forsaken by God, we see the reason that *we* are *never* forsaken by God (note Josh. 1:5; Heb. 13:5). For Jesus was forsaken so that you and I never have to be.

Whole-Bible Connections

DARKNESS AND LIGHT. In the beginning, darkness covered the earth (Gen. 1:2). God created light (Gen. 1:3–5) and called his people, the children of Abraham, to be "a light for the nations," bringing blessing and peace to the world (Isa. 42:6; 49:6; 60:3). Darkness, on the other hand, represented divine judgment (Ex. 10:21–23) and lament (Amos 8:9–10). When Jesus died on the cross, once more, as in Genesis 1:2, "there was darkness over the whole land" (Mark 15:33). In this way God was judging all sin and unrighteousness. He was doing more than this, though. He was re-creating. He was starting over. The death and resurrection of Jesus marked a new creation (2 Cor. 5:17–6:2). And once more, God separated light from darkness, calling his people to be light in a dark world (Eph. 5:8; 1 Thess. 5:5; 1 Pet. 2:9; 1 John 2:8–9). One day, in the new earth, the nations will walk in the light of the Lamb, whose bright shining eliminates the need for the sun (Rev. 21:22–26).

SON OF GOD. "Truly this man was the Son of God!" (Mark 15:39). The great hope of the Old Testament is the coming of a deliverer, a king, a Messiah (which means "anointed one," i.e., king), who would rescue the people of God and usher in God's glorious kingdom once and for all. This king was called God's "son" in the Old Testament (e.g., 2 Sam. 7:13–14; Psalm 2). When this Messiah finally showed up, however, it slowly became evident to his followers that he was more than a mere man. He walked on water, forgave sins, and identified himself as the true temple—all things that only God himself can do. Thus in Mark 15:39, when the centurion exclaims that Jesus was the Son of God, we are to join the centurion in seeing that Jesus is not only the Son of God in that he is the Messiah, but also that he is the Son of God in that he is divine.

Theological Soundings

ATONEMENT. "And they crucified him . . ." (Mark 15:24). The Bible teaches that in Jesus' death on the cross, he suffered the penalty for all the sins of his people as their substitute. Theologians call this *penal substitutionary atonement*: Jesus paid sin's penalty (penal) in our place (substitutionary) to restore us to God (atonement). Perhaps the single clearest verse explaining what Jesus did in the event narrated in Mark 15 is 1 Peter 3:18, which says that Christ "suffered once for sins [penal], the righteous for the unrighteous [substitutionary], that he might bring us to God [atonement]." As we look in trusting faith to Christ, this atonement becomes effectual for us, and we are restored to God as his beloved children.

RESURRECTION. "He has risen," said the angel, "he is not here" (Mark 16:6). Three times throughout Mark, Jesus had said that he would suffer and rise on the third day (Mark 8:31; 9:31; 10:34). Christ's resurrection had implications for himself, for history, and for his people. First, for Christ himself, his resurrection vindicated him and established him as the Messiah he claimed to be (Rom. 1:4). Second, regarding history, Jesus' resurrection fulfills God's promises to raise up and restore Israel (Hos. 6:1–3), for Jesus embodied in himself true Israel (remember, for example, his testing in the wilderness, succeeding where Israel had failed [Matt. 4:1–11]). And third, as the "firstfruits" of the resurrection, Jesus in his raised body is the first instance of the new order of humanity in which believers are promised to participate in the new earth (1 Cor. 15:20–22).

> ### Personal Implications

Take time to reflect on the implications of Mark 15:16–16:8 for your own life today. Make notes below on the personal implications for your walk with the Lord of (1) the *Gospel Glimpses*, (2) the *Whole-Bible Connections*, (3) the *Theological Soundings*, and (4) this passage as a whole.

1. Gospel Glimpses

---

2. Whole-Bible Connections

---

3. Theological Soundings

4. Mark 15:16–16:8

Take a moment now to ask for the Lord's blessing and help as you continue in this study of Mark. And take a moment also to look back through this unit of study, to reflect on a few key things that the Lord may be teaching you—and perhaps to highlight or underline these to review again in the future.

Definitions

[1] **Crucifixion** – A means of execution in which the person was fastened, by ropes or nails, to a crossbeam that was then raised and attached to a vertical beam, forming a cross (the root meaning of "crucifixion"). The process was designed to maximize pain and humiliation, and to serve as a deterrent for other potential offenders. Jesus suffered this form of execution, not for any offense he had committed (Heb. 4:15) but as the atoning sacrifice for all who would believe in him (Mark 10:45; John 3:16).

[2] **Sacrifice** – An offering to God, often to signify forgiveness of sin. The Law of Moses gave detailed instructions regarding various kinds of sacrifices.

[3] **Anoint** – In Scripture, to pour oil (usually olive oil) on someone or something to set the person or thing apart for a special purpose. (The Hebrew word *Messiah* and its Greek equivalent *Christ* both mean "anointed one.") In Mark 16:1, the women anoint Jesus' body as part of the embalming process.

WEEK 12: SUMMARY AND CONCLUSION

As we draw this study of Mark to a close, we begin by summing up the big picture of Mark as a whole. We will then review some questions for reflection in light of Mark's entire account, with a final identification of Gospel Glimpses, Whole-Bible Connections, and Theological Soundings, all with a view to appreciating the Gospel of Mark in its entirety.

The Big Picture of Mark

Over the course of this study we have seen that Mark's Gospel falls roughly into two halves.

The first half (1:1–8:30) shows Jesus performing miracles, gathering disciples, teaching about God's kingdom, and amazing crowds. In short, he is convincing the disciples that he is indeed the long-awaited king, the Messiah.

The second half of Mark (8:31–16:8) shows Jesus suddenly and repeatedly predicting his suffering and death as he shows his disciples what kind of king he is going to be. He is to be a suffering king. And Jesus repeatedly connects this suffering of his to the life of his disciples. Yet this suffering will, as for Jesus, lead ultimately to life and glory for his faithful disciples.

Putting both halves together, the Gospel of Mark shows us that in Jesus, God has provided redemption for his people. Jesus came as the fulfillment of the Old Testament promises for a coming king. He was not the king they expected (a king of political triumph); he was the king they most desperately needed (a king of suffering). The kingdom of God arrived, and with it its rightful ruler (Mark 1:14–15). But this ruler laid down "his life as a ransom for many" (Mark 10:45). By faith in Jesus and his work on our behalf, we are restored to God and enter into God's kingdom. The first half of Mark shows us that God has come to us. The second half shows us how we can come to God. (For further background, see the *ESV Study Bible*, pages 1889–1892; also online at www.esv.org.)

Read through the following three sections on *Gospel Glimpses*, *Whole-Bible Connections*, and *Theological Soundings*. Then take time to reflect on the *Personal Implications* these sections may have for your walk with the Lord.

Gospel Glimpses

Throughout Mark we have seen the grace of God in the gospel. Jesus has shown mercy to sinners, shared meals with the socially marginalized, and touched the ceremonially unclean. He has exposed and confounded the emptiness of the religion of the scribes and Pharisees, earning their opposition as a result. Time and again Jesus has upended our intuitive expectations as to who receives the attention of God and who does not. Throughout, we are reminded that God's mercy benefits just those who know their need of it. The reason this can be so is Jesus' death on our behalf: "the Son of Man came not to be served but to serve, and to give his life as a ransom for many" (10:45).

Has your understanding of the gospel changed at all during the course of this study?

Are there any particular passages in Mark that have brought the gospel home to you in a fresh way?

Whole-Bible Connections

While Mark does not often quote the Old Testament explicitly, his Gospel is filled with allusions to the Old Testament (think, for example, of the story of Jonah as a backdrop to Mark 4:35–41). More than this, Mark uses the categories and language of the Old Testament—referring to the temple, a fig tree, a vineyard, the Son of Man, Moses, Elijah, and much more. Throughout, we see in Mark that Jesus is bringing the entire Old Testament to decisive fulfillment—as Jesus says in Mark 1:15, "The time is fulfilled." Jesus is the one who, through his death and resurrection, is leading God's people to their true restoration, their final exodus, their needed liberation.

How has your understanding of the place of Mark in the sweep of the Bible been deepened through your study of Mark?

What are some connections in Mark to the Old Testament that you hadn't noticed before?

Has your understanding of the unity of the Bible been clarified through studying Mark? How so?

What development has there been in your view of who Jesus is and how he fulfills the Old Testament?

Theological Soundings

Mark contributes much to Christian theology. Doctrines that are reinforced and clarified in Mark include the deity of Christ, human sin, resurrection, divine sovereignty, and the kingdom of God.

Where has your theology been tweaked or corrected as you have studied Mark?

How might our understanding of God be impoverished if we did not have Mark's Gospel?

How does Mark's Gospel uniquely contribute to our understanding of Jesus?

Are there any specific ways in which Mark helps us understand the human condition?

Personal Implications

As you consider the Gospel of Mark as a whole, what implications do you see for your own life? Consider especially the issue of discipleship. This is an important emphasis throughout Mark, particularly chapters 8–10. What are the ramifications for your own life of Jesus' teaching on discipleship in Mark?

As You Finish Studying Mark . . .

We rejoice with you as you finish studying the book of Mark! May this study become part of your Christian walk of faith, day by day and week by week throughout all your life. Now we would greatly encourage you to continue to study the Word of God on a week-by-week basis. To continue your study of the Bible, we would encourage you to consider other books in the *Knowing the Bible* series, and to visit www.knowingthebibleseries.org.

Lastly, take a moment again to look back through this book of Mark, which you have studied during these recent weeks. Review again the notes that you have written, and the things that you have highlighted or underlined. Reflect again on the key themes that the Lord has been teaching you about himself and about his Word. May these things become a treasure for you throughout your life—which we pray will be true for you, in the name of the Father, and the Son, and the Holy Spirit. Amen.